Marlbro
Books

4-3-64

(458-4977)

PÉTAIN

PÉTAIN

GLORNEY BOLTON

Ruskin House
GEORGE ALLEN & UNWIN LTD
MUSEUM STREET LONDON

FIRST PUBLISHED IN 1957

TO LEWIS WAY

Printed in Great Britain
in 12 pt Fournier type
by SIMSON SHAND LTD
London, Hertford and Harlow

PREFACE

ON an autumnal Sunday afternoon in 1955 I entered the Dauphine's apartment in the Château of Versailles. Like many others, I had come to see an exhibition which marked the life of Queen Marie-Antoinette, born two hundred years ago. As we walked through one spacious room after another, the furniture awaiting our gaze increased in splendour and elegance. Portraits assumed the quickening touch of the flesh. The old charm of royalty swept back the republican years; and the visitors, hitherto baffled by the unfamiliar *juvenilia* of Schoenbrunn, expressed delight in the jewellery worn by a Queen of France and in the letters which had been written to her by an understanding Swedish lover. The flow of history sparkled into life.

Two large drawings conveyed the throb of excitement when, in 1782, King Louis the Sixteenth and his consort visited Paris in state. Never before or since, it seems, have a King and a Queen won such fervour of love from a multitude; and within a decade all was changed. In the last room the Queen, now 'widow Capet', is seen mounting the platform of the guillotine. To the brutal end she keeps her dignity.

Few visitors to the exhibition in Versailles that Sunday afternoon walked away from the exhibition unmoved; for we had seen the life and the times of a Queen re-enacted. Marie-Antoinette was a dainty, frolicsome child of the eighteenth century, and in her unexpected suffering she reached greatness. Those passions and hatreds which stole the minds of Frenchmen more than three half-centuries ago are smouldering or dead. Pity alone is active. The crowd in the Dauphine's apartment forgot their own descent from revolutionary accusers, judges and executioners. The Bourbons no longer deserved to rule; nor did they deserve violently to die. Revolution would have become all the more glorious if, as ostensibly in England, it had been bloodless. The French are charitable to Queen Marie-Antoinette and to the frivolous sinners of another age, but passions and hatreds find new objects. A courteous gentleman begged me to pass through the turnstile before him. What were his loyalties a dozen years ago—Pétainist or Gaullist? The pitying crowd might be still dangerously divided.

In the war years I worked closely with the Czech leaders, Eduard Benes and Jan Masaryk. I was bound, therefore, to know other Continental exiles in London: the Poles, the Yugoslavs, the Greeks, the Norwegians, the Belgians and the Fighting French. There were many formal parties which exiled monarchs or presidents attended, and 'Excellencies' seemed to be as plentiful as the chorus-girls of a Cochran show. Yet one leader, while exiled in London, was persistently denied the diplomatic honours due to a president or minister of State; and he—Charles de Gaulle—was the greatest of them all. Why was he held back while the Presidents of Czechoslovakia and Poland signed pacts with each other and maintained their legations and consulates in the Allied or neutral countries? This answer was bound up with the status of Marshal Pétain. This ancient man, despite his imperfect sympathy with our country, never became its deliberate enemy.

He was born a peasant, and at heart he remained a peasant to the end of his long life. On the eve of war in 1914, he was 58; he had never seen a battle, and he expected soon to retire. The conflict proved that his own unfashionable views on a war of attrition were right, and he rose quickly to the rank of general. Joffre sent him to Verdun almost as an afterthought. It was an exacting command for one who never forgot that the soldier is made of flesh and nerves and that his powers of endurance are limited. He hated to see a single life needlessly destroyed. He quelled a grim mutiny by going to the roots of the soldiers' grievances, and the number of death sentences which, as Commander-in-Chief, he authorized did not exceed twenty-six.

No other commander, not even Foch, drew so strong an affection from the millions who had stood knee-deep in the mud of the
trenches. The affection was magnified as the years of the Great
War receded. Outliving Joffre, Gallieni, Foch and the bellicose
civilian, Clemenceau, the 'hero of Verdun' became the personal
embodiment of fighting France; at his introduction to the French
Academy Paul Valéry called him 'the spirit of the resistance'. He
was a legend, and legends deceive. Daladier made him Ambassador
to Spain when Franco had won the civil war. Reynaud made him
Vice-President of the Council when the German tanks were about
to sweep into France. In the hour of swift defeat President Lebrun
asked him to succeed Reynaud as Prime Minister. Each forgot that
old age knows no real escape from physical and mental decay.
These appointments with destiny were made because the people
wanted them.

From the Embassy in Madrid Pétain studied the lightning war
on Poland and read the reports of the Nazi or Soviet subjection of
a beaten people. The fear haunted him that France might become
a second Poland; and, called back to Paris when the defences were
already broken, he formed the resolve never to leave the homeland.
It was useless, he believed, to renew the struggle from North
Africa. 'If we abandon France', he told a harassed and divided
Cabinet, 'we may never find her again.' No sooner had he become
Prime Minister than he begged for peace, and the only armistice
which Hitler ever made was with the French. If, through vanity,
expediency or political conviction, Pétain put the legislature of the
Third Republic into cold storage and got himself proclaimed Head
of the State, he had the open support of a big majority in the
National Assembly; and, at his trial for high treason, his counsel
claimed juridically that the court had no authority to try him,
since he was the Head of the State and remained so until the
National Assembly met to take away his powers.

No doubt, like General Weygand and most of his countrymen,
he was once convinced that Britain must soon follow the French
example and sue for peace; but, as an old master of war, he never

failed to detect each turning of the tide, and in his own heart he echoed the words of de Gaulle that France had lost a battle, and not a war. When the Americans had landed in North Africa, many wanted him immediately to leave France. An aeroplane was ready. On African soil Pétainist and Gaullist might sink their differences to fight the more resolutely against their common enemy, the German invader. Pétain stayed with the people. 'I give my glory,' he said.

Glory was certainly torn to shreds. The whole country felt the weight of the crooked cross. Shamefaced ministers became the helpless tools of an alien police State. Within twenty months Pétain was taken away from Vichy, a prisoner of the Germans. On his eighty-ninth birthday he was arrested by French officers. He stood on trial for his life and, like Napoleon, he spent his six last years as a captive on a lonely island.

Marshal Juin, faithful to Pétain until Darlan released him from his oath, loves France. So did Marshal de Lattre de Tassigny, once submissive to the yoke of Vichy. General de Gaulle, eloquent in deeds, as in the spoken and the written word, loves the idea of France. Pétain loved the people of France. In one aspect or another, love of France dominated all the actors, high-minded or shabby, in a tragic episode. We are not bound to think of Pétain as King Lear who, unaccountably, chose Iago for his prompter. In tragic life, Meredith has written, 'no villain need be'. Passions spun the plot: so did suspicions, fears and honest intentions cruelly flouted.

The men of Vichy and the men of the Resistance pour out their memoirs. Already the documentation is immense, and the debate will not be ended in our lifetime. Pétain—the chief figure-head, if not the chief actor, in the drama—speaks from the grave. He had his reasons for what he did and for what he suffered. He was the spokesman, but never the master, of beaten France. For a full four years the master of France was Hitler.

Hitler was also the master of disrupted Czechoslovakia. While I worked with the exiled Czechs in London, I thought often of their tormented compatriots in the Bohemian homeland. It was easy to be defiant in London and hard to be gallant under the shadow of the Gestapo in Paris or in Prague. Open defiance was too often foolhardy. We have obligations to our allies, but loyalty to the Motherland comes first. Though there were many time-servers in Prague or Vichy, some were genuinely anxious to ensure the survival of their own country. They had what Pétain himself called 'a long patience'. Their resistance was not gallant, like de Gaulle's, nor open-handed, like Mahatma Gandhi's against the British, but they were not devoid of patriotism. In their own way they waged a war of attrition against the conqueror.

Joan of Arc was vindicated twenty-five years after her agonizing death. Alfred Dreyfus was mercifully vindicated in his own lifetime. It is impossible that the verdict given at the end of Pétain's long trial will go unchallenged. Yet I do not pretend to offer a vindication. There are incidents in the Vichy record which make the blood run cold; but all were confused by the swift-moving events of the summer of 1940. We understand Pétain's actions better when we have first found out what manner of man he was. We should study him in his strength and in his weakness: the tenacity of purpose and the disabling pessimism; the fine sweep of a military mind and the political ineptitude; the glorious legend and the enfeebled grandeur of old age. At 84, when he was called to rule, Marshal Pétain could neither change his character nor his habits of mind, France chose him, and France condemned him, and his tragedy gives flesh and tortured nerve to the tragedy of a whole generation. One day the errors will be forgiven, like those of Queen Marie-Antoinette. Pity will triumph.

The *verbatim* reports of Pétain's trial were a principal source of information. I have quarried from General Laure's biography of the Marshal as well as from Captain Liddell Hart's biographical studies of Foch and other leaders of the first World War. Of English writers on France's tribulations in 1940 I found General Spears the most persuasive. The chief authority on Pétain's last years on the Ile d'Yeu is M. Jaques Isorni. He and

M. Jean Lamaire defended the Marshal at his trial, and they worked magnanimously for his rehabilitation.

CONTENTS

CONTENTS

CHAPTER ONE

SOLDIER OF THE REPUBLIC

ASTRIDE the military road from Arras to St Omer stands the small village of Cauchy-la-Tour, where Philippe Pétain, a peasant's son, was born on April 24, 1856. He was the fourth of seven children, and he lost his mother when he was still an infant. The father soon married again, and Philippe, starved of affection, grew up reticent and shy. One man alone knew how to draw him out, and that was his mother's uncle, the Abbé Léfèbre. The old priest had served in the Grand Army under the great Napoleon. He liked to talk of his fighting past, but he remembered that many evil things were done through callousness or neglect. The Grand Army was formed of flesh and blood. It was body and soul; and the Abbé had seen the flesh mercilessly torn, the body broken by stupid commands. Nearly all the men with whom he talked were simple and dour. He knew the elemental justice of their cursing and swearing, and he was a tender confessor.

He urged the family to send his great-nephew to St Bertin's College, a Dominican foundation, in St Omer. There Philippe learned to write with a firm hand. He expressed himself accurately, and in mathematics he was known to outstrip his teachers. His gestures, like his words, were few. Yet he had a restless energy, and whenever he walked with the other boys past the former Cathedral of Nôtre Dame and along the banks of the canal, his light blue eyes steadily took in all that was to be seen.

Close to the college was the military depot and recruiting station, which young men entered, often unwillingly, to don the Emperor's uniform. One day Philippe saw a troop of Light Horse prancing into the narrow street. The glitter of sword-buckle and helmet, the gay tunics, the easy horsemanship delighted him, and he cried: 'I will be a Light Horseman.' But before he had a chance to talk things over with the Abbé Léfèbre, now nearly ninety, the college closed its doors. France was at war with Prussia.

The fever of war soon spread from Paris to battle-scarred St Omer, and in their mess-room officers drank to the day when they should meet again in Berlin. In that distant city, they said, the Emperor would impose a peace restoring to France the left bank of the Rhine. It was hers by right and by nature; for nature had marked out the boundaries of France. 'We shall reach them,' Danton once told the Convention, 'at their four ends, at the ocean, at the banks of the Rhine, at the Alps, at the Pyrenees. No power can stop us.' Napoleon won the left bank for France, and the peacemakers who were her foes took it away. Now war had come again, and the fighting men of France set out quickly to settle the future of the Rhine.

The war was swift, but, instead of resounding victory, it brought defeat. The Emperor, mortally sick and wracked with pain, acted for a whole month as his own Commander-in-Chief. When he divested these powers and gave them to the brave but cautious Marshal Bazaine, it was already too late. The French had the better weapons, but the Prussians, who had the better plan, struck two crippling blows. At Sedan they cut off the forces under Marshal MacMahon and made the Emperor their prisoner. At Metz they broke the resistance of Marshal Bazaine. 'Metz has capitulated,' Gambetta told the people. 'Bazaine has committed treason.'

Army had defeated army. A campaign was virtually over. Bismarck swaggered into the Palace of Versailles to proclaim the King of Prussia as the German Emperor. The victor took for his main prize the whole province of Alsace and a large portion of the province of Lorraine. In vain spokesmen of the ceded provinces told the Assembly in Bordeaux that they did not want to be the subjects of the new German Emperor, and in vain the exiled Empress Eugénie made her appeal to Potsdam. 'I love my country as you love yours,' the German Emperor told her. 'Therefore, I understand the bitter feelings which fill the heart of Your Majesty. But Germany, having made enormous sacrifices for her defences, wants to make sure that the next war will find her better equipped to repulse the attack with which we have to reckon as soon as France will have recovered her strength. It is this sad consideration alone which compels me to insist on cessions of land which serve no purpose but to remove the starting point of the French army farther back for the future.'

The German Emperor forged one more link in the chain-war of Europe, for he touched the nerve of a nation's pride. The taking of the left bank of the Rhine had been a dream chiefly for French officers in pursuit of military glory, but when an enemy seized two fair provinces he trespassed upon the soil of France. Philippe Pétain, in common with many thousands of other peasant lads, felt the hurt. The wells of strength were in the husbandmen of France. They haggled over each *sou*. They kept watch against each sport or freak of nature. They were calculating, close-fisted, cunning; and they moved stubbornly within the perpetual cycle of sowing and harvesting. By pain, sweat and exhaustive care they made the earth of France resplendent with fruit and worthy of defence. Tomorrow's war would be peasantry on the march.

Peace played strange tricks with the reputations of the war leaders. The Emperor died an exile in England, Marshal MacMahon became President of the Republic, and Marshal Bazaine left Geneva to demand a public inquiry into his military conduct. He was born a man of the people, and he believed that society was taking its revenge. The people, he once told his sister, believe anything. 'I cannot deny my humble origin; and no doubt it is because I come from the people and from the ranks that jealousy pursues me, especially since I was made a Marshal. Officers from the Special Schools cannot forgive it.'

The Assembly did as he wished, and a Marshal of France was put on trial. He was indicted on three explicit charges. He had capitulated at Metz without exhausting all the means of defence; he had capitulated with an army in the field; he had negotiated with the enemy before doing everything that was required by duty and honour. Yet he was certain that he had a complete answer to each charge. The trial took place at the Grand Trianon in Versailles, and seven weeks passed before the last witness gave his evidence. The Marshal was found guilty and sentenced to death. He expected to be shot; but the President of the Republic, showing mercy to a brother-officer, changed the death sentence to imprisonment for twenty years. Bazaine was taken to the island fortress of St Marguerite, midway between Cannes and Cap d'Antibes, and after about eight months he escaped to Genoa.

Meanwhile a new generation was coming to manhood. War had shown the stark need for a larger army and for many more well-trained reservists. Despite the punishment awaiting Bazaine, youths of little social standing were soon encouraged to take up the profession of arms, and at seventeen Pétain left St Bertin's College for the Military School in Nancy. Only a few miles away stood the posts marking the new German frontier. Its proximity haunted all living in the city which Pétain came to love.

Sometimes, from the pulpit of a garrison church, he heard praises of Joan, the peasant girl who left the neighbouring village of Domrémy to lead a wretched prince to Rheims for his consecration and crowning as the King of France. As soon as her strange mission was done fortune deserted her. Through treachery she was taken prisoner at Compiègne. The Holy Inquisition and the far-famed University of Paris joined in her condemnation, and she was put to death. 'We are lost,' cried an English soldier who watched her dying. 'We have burned a saint.'

He was right. The tide turned against his countrymen, and when at last peace came to a stricken land, Calais was the only possession left to them across the Channel. Joan's mother, knowing that an innocent had died, never gave up her quest for a revision of the trial. The common people encouraged her, and slowly a lethargic King realized that he owed his coronation to a peasant girl. Authority tarnished his kingship each time it called her a heretic. Thus, twenty-five years after her death, the girl won a legal rehabilitation. The trial in Rouen was declared irregular and its judgment was reversed.

In the end the truth prevails. Justice is done. It followed that one day Lorraine, the maid's province, would be restored to France. That was the moral of the tale told from the pulpit. Most youths at the Military School in Nancy believed it to be true. Pétain, trained to be a good Catholic, was only too willing to share the neighbourhood's devotion to Joan's memory. None the less, he preferred hard calculation to intuition, and already his studies had taught him that, in large measure, the expulsion of the English from France was due to the use of artillery.

At 20 he entered St Cyr. This military academy gave outward loyalty to the new Republic, though, perhaps, not a single member of its teaching staff was yet a genuine republican. Each felt himself to be committed by the shame of defeat, and each lived for the past. So, too, did Marshal MacMahon, and though he had agreed to be President of the Republic, he kept his heart royalist. He knew that if only the royalists of France—the Bourbonists, the Orleanists and the Bonapartists—had agreed upon the choice of a King, the dreaded Third Republic would not have come into existence; and he longed for the day when, as an Orleanist, he might surrender his authority to the Comte de Paris. Friends shunned him because they would have nothing to do with the Republic. Yet they believed that it was their Christian duty to defend France against her external enemies; and thus they allowed their sons to go to St Cyr and to obtain their commissions in a republican army.

Since the Republic was an evil creation, the monarchists were certain that it would not endure. One day the swords of a new generation of officers might be wanted for the defence of throne and altar. It was well, therefore, to keep the profession of arms exclusive; and while the Ministry of War widened the area of recruitment for officers, the spirit of the military clans made steeper the gradations of society.

B

MacMahon had been President for less than a year when Pétain first entered St Cyr. The new cadet was a believer, but without a shred of social influence. Outwardly he shared the life of his military companions. Yet he did nothing to hide his lowly origin. He had no fashionable friends, and he was too poor to make any of the customary expeditions into Paris. Solitude, however, had no terrors for him, for a motherless childhood taught him how to be self-reliant. He was a listener, not a talker. When his two years at St Cyr were drawing to a close, he might be seen helping new cadets over their difficulties, but with cadets of his own seniority he often showed a forbidding silence. He had painfully to learn the ways of the great world, and whenever he broke his silence with a phrase of biting sarcasm he made himself unpopular.

He found relief from his loneliness not in rebellion, but in superb efficiency. He used his gifts of intellect proudly. His written work was clear, if excessively painstaking, and whatever instructors thought of his social bearing, they knew that he was alert and soldierly. Only a few months after he had been posted to Villefranche as a second lieutenant in the 24th Batallion of Infantry he was sent to the School of Musketry at Valbonne, where he was soon known as a 'clever rifleman'. Meanwhile he matched his industry at the rifle range and in the lecture hall with strenuous physical exercises. He worked out these exercises in his own matter-of-fact way, and though they were not deliberately designed for grace or harmony, he became the most agile young officer at Valbonne. He jumped walls and gates with ease, and he gave his muscles the firmness of steel. He was thus magnificently prepared for the day when he was granted his wish to join a special Alpine corps.

For the next five years he studied the science of mountain warfare. One day the enemy might seep through the Alps, the Vosges or the Pyrenees, and Pétain learned how to fight him on perilous heights. From Mentone or Sospel he led his men on long journeys to awkward bastions. They lived surrounded by snow and crags. One soldier's strength was pitted against another's, and inevitably the distinctions of the barrack-square were relaxed. Officers were compelled to live more on a level with their men, and with his own eyes Pétain saw the need of making sure that they were properly fed and clothed. Grievances had to be heeded promptly. Pétain showed little inclination to leave the Alpine corps. Even its remoteness from the great world appealed to him; but his brain was as tireless as his body, and his curiosity about fire-power, first roused at Valbonne, could not be quenched. Favourable reports of his work, moreover, continued to reach the Ministry of War. At 32 he entered the Staff College.

If at St Cyr Pétain had to battle with snobberies accentuated by defeat in war, at the Staff College he faced a teaching that was formidable and new to French minds. It was the doctrine of Clausewitz, the real victor of Sedan and Metz; for a quiet-mannered Prussian, born nine years before the French Revolution began, had created his own revolution in the science of war. He proclaimed the will to conquer, the primacy of the offensive and the cardinal importance of striking the enemy at his heart.

His teaching was opposed to nearly all the military thought of the century in which he was born. 'I am not in favour of giving battle, especially at the outset of war,' Marshal Saxe wrote in 1757. 'I am ever convinced that an able general can wage war his whole life without being compelled to do so.' A good general, he believed, first weakens and then upsets the enemy by frequent encounters. 'Decline the attack altogether,' he added, 'unless you can make it with advantage.' Pierre de Bourcet taught that an army has limbs: it ought to move freely while seeking to cut off, or to paralyse, the outer limbs of his foes. When Frederick the Great ordered his troops to volley their fire as they advanced, the Comte de Guibert observed that firing was better aimed when soldiers were stationary. 'This type of fire', he wrote, 'is the most lively and slaughtering of any; it stimulates the soldier; it makes him insensible to danger; it suits the address and vivacity of the French.'

For the French once knew the arts of defensive warfare. A few

weeks before Austerlitz Napoleon, himself a child of the eighteenth century, said: 'All my care will be to gain victory with the
least possible shedding of blood; my soldiers are my children.'
But Clausewitz wrote: 'Let us not hear of generals who conquer
without bloodshed'; and his chief disciple happened to be the
great Prussian commander, Helmuth von Moltke. Thus Prussia's
war on Austria in 1866 was the first of the Clausewitzian wars, and
her war on France was the second. By striking the enemy at the
heart she made his defeat in the field quick and overwhelming.

Then came Clausewitz's third victory: he converted the beaten
French. Their generals talked incessantly of the attack. They began to scorn the importance of weapon-power because their own
superiority in weapons had not frustrated the onslaught of the
Prussians. No longer did the generals heed Napoleon's words to
'read and re-read the campaigns of the Great Captains'. Clausewitz was the successful revolutionary, and the defensive tradition
of the French Army was thrown away.

Clausewitz deceived the French, but not the shrewd von
Moltke. On the contrary, his two wars taught him that the doctrine
had some serious shortcomings. In old age he worked out a plan
for a double attack on France and Russia, and it was on lines which
Clausewitz would not have approved. In France, too, there arose
differing interpretations of the doctrine, and Pétain, as he scanned
the text, soon realized that the hard core of the doctrine was
hedged with many reservations. The attack must rest on sureness
and security. Pétain found nothing in Clausewitz's arguments to
excuse a lack of fire-power, and the conviction grew stronger that
good weapons were needed as much for defence as for attack.

Pétain's taut and practical intelligence attracted the attention
of the two ablest teachers at the Staff College. One was Colonel
Bonnal, an authority on Napoleon's methods of warfare, and the
other was Colonel Millet, a Protestant. Millet was distressed by an
ever-increasing friction between Catholic and anti-clerical. Waves
of suspicion and hatred swept through the Staff College and the
military academies to lash officers who, like Pétain, were neither

freethinkers nor upholders of social privilege. They warped men's judgments and might dangerously divide a nation which needs unity in the face of an external foe. The Staff College, Millet argued, existed to train leaders in war, not partisans; and he sought out officers who, whatever their religious background or convictions may have been, knew how to give their minds boldly to the problems of France's defence. He shared with Bonnal the belief that Pétain would go far.

Yet their pupil, on leaving the Staff College, was still without influence. Promotion limped slowly towards him, and more than once the post for which he was fitted went to an officer more familiar with the ways of the Third Republic or a military clique. He had, moreover, an uncompromising sense of military discipline, and it might have brought his career to shipwreck when he was a company commander at Vincennes. In his company was Professor Mirman, who, at 30, was doing a belated year of military service. Mirman was also a deputy and jealous of his status within the Republic. He obtained leave and went to Paris, where he spoke in the Chamber on a matter which, Pétain insisted, did not concern his barrack-room duties. The commander, therefore, ordered the deputy to be detained. This incident at Vincennes, already famed for the execution of the Duc d'Enghien, might easily have provoked a storm in the Chamber; but Mirman accepted his plight with amused detachment, and he bore Pétain no grudge.

The years of the long peace dragged on, but they would not last for ever. In an Alpine Corps Pétain learned how to defend his country against an enemy coming through the mountains, and when Captain Marchand planted the tricolour in the remote African village of Fashoda, all Europe realized how precarious was the friendship between France and England. Vigilantly Pétain learned English as well as German. The French, he decided, must be more inventive than their neighbours, and in 1899 he became an air-balloon officer. It was exactly a century after Napoleon had disbanded an air-balloon corps set up by the army of the Revolution.

Early in the new century life was still obscure for Major Pétain, but Millet, now a general, had not forgotten him. He had gone to the Ministry of War as Director of Infantry, and soon he was troubled by the antiquated teaching on musketry. In his eyes the chief offender was the School of Musketry in Chalons, where young officers were taught how to fire in groups and to spray their fire over the ground. Their commandant told them repeatedly that collective firing was more important than individual firing. An army, he was sure, could have too many good riflemen rather than too few, and thus the School neglected to give the rifleman his individual training. Millet decided to deal first with the chief offender and, recalling his former pupil's sure-footed knowledge of fire-power, he sent Pétain to Chalons to reform its doctrine.

The commandant gave him a cold reception. He sat at a large table with three or four senior officers and called sharply for a statement. Pétain answered frigidly with dryness. Without the slightest pretence to charm or ease of manner he unfolded his arguments for the intensive training of the rifleman and explained the severe discipline to which he must submit. The commandant did not argue, for there was nothing to be said. He had a stronger aid than argument. First he intrigued for Millet's removal from the Ministry of War, and when he had succeeded he convinced a new Director of Infantry that Pétain must be promptly transferred from Chalons. A discredited reformer went back to barracks. But Bonnal heard of his plight, and he was now Director of the Staff College and a general. Within six months he made the advocate of fire-power an assistant professor of Infantry Tactics.

Pétain went back to a familiar building, but he also stepped into a new epoch. The day of the royalists, secret or avowed, was at an end, and now the Minister of War, General André, was busily removing from the key-positions of the Army all ultramontane Catholics and royalists. He was soon casting his anti-clerical net over the Staff College, and he discovered that Major Foch, another assistant professor, was the brother of a Jesuit. Ferdinand Foch, an imaginative Celt from the Pyrennes, was still a student at the Jesuit College in Metz when he saw the Emperor, a doomed man, in front of the Prefecture. He had watched officers entering and leaving the Grand Hotel, where Bazaine installed his staff; 'the general was playing billiards'. Soon afterwards the College closed its doors. Foch went home, and at St Etienne he enlisted. He was still tediously drilling when the swift war ended.

He returned to the classroom desk in Metz. A few weeks went by, and suddenly he heard a salvo fired by the German gunners at the fort. Like all the other youths, he jumped to his feet; for the salvo told them the terrible news that Bismarck and Jules Faure had signed a peace treaty. The ground on which they now stood had become German. The boys looked at their superintendent. 'Mes enfants,' he said quietly, and there was a long silence. Foch made the silence a dedication. Lorraine, the maid's province, must be won back for France.

General André removed the Jesuit's brother from the Staff College and sent him to Laon, where a Protestant would be his superior officer. The Protestant was none other than Millet, and he took away the sting of the Minister's studied affront to a Catholic. Each of the two officers had known shabby treatment, and each gave his mind to the recurring war. The anti-clerical scourge afflicted many other officers; but whenever one of them told Foch that he thought seriously of resigning his commission, he heard a ready answer. 'You have no pluck,' Foch would say. 'When war comes you will have to put up with worse things than that. If you can't stand it now, what will you do then?' And each morning he leaped on his horse to show that he was ready for the cavalry charge.

It was not without anxiety, therefore, that Pétain took up his post at the Staff College. He expected rebuffs and, like Foch, he was ready to meet them calmly. He seldom, if ever, committed his private thoughts to paper. He was not, like Foch, a man of intuition and faith. His mind was hard, calculating, practical. For some years, it was said, he gave up going to Mass. He was not a stalwart of throne and altar; nor was he a lover of the Chamber of Deputies. He lived in a soldier's world; and while he wanted many more direct and simpler contacts between officers and their men, he accepted a military system that was hierarchic.

A decade before Pétain went back to the Staff College Pope Leo XIII issued an encyclical in which he asked the faithful of France to serve the Republic. It was their duty, he reminded them, to work with an admittedly imperfect government. If the Pope had his way men like Pétain would have lived both as good Catholics and as loyal Republicans. Events were to make that way almost too hard, for a cruel injustice was setting family against family. It led directly to the purges within the Army, turning the persecutors of one year into the persecuted of another. The secret trial, degradation and banishment of an innocent Jew seared the conscience of the entire nation.

In October 1894, the *Libre Parole*, an anti-Semitic journal, announced that Captain Alfred Dreyfus, a member of the General Staff, had been arrested on a charge of selling military secrets to a foreign Power. A Jew with a German name, the journal told its readers, sold the secrets to Germany. The report was soon confirmed by General Mercier, Minister of War, and he added that the Government had proofs of his treason. Within a week of Christmas Dreyfus faced a secret trial in a military courtroom. He was found guilty and condemned to lifelong imprisonment. In the New Year a furious crowd watched the harsh ceremong of his degradation and expulsion from the Army. He was sent to Devil's Island, a hideous place of confinement off New Guinea.

The crowd which witnessed his humiliation reflected the anger of nearly all their countrymen. Socialists, ranged for once on the side of the royalists, argued that Dreyfus would certainly have been shot if he were a peasant, and not the member of a rich Jewish family. One man alone was convinced of his innocence, and that was his brother, Mathieu Dreyfus. The condemned man's brother, like the mother of Joan, knew no peace of mind until he had won his self-chosen battle for justice.

Two years after the secret trial Colonel Picquart became the head of the Intelligence Branch of the General Staff. He decided to

study the *bordereau*, or list of documents which had passed to the
German military attaché, and he began to doubt whether the handwriting of the *bordereau* was that of Dreyfus. He suspected that it
was the handwriting of an officer senior to Dreyfus. As a man of
severe Calvinistic upbringing, he could not keep his suspicions to
himself, and he talked things over with his chief. Picquart was a
danger, and when he persisted in asking for an investigation, the
Ministry of War sent him away to Africa.

His successor, Colonel Henry, waited until Picquart was out of
France, and then he released fascimilies of the *bordereau* which had
brought Dreyfus to his doom. The newspapers were allowed to
use them as photographs. It was a fatal step. A bank manager, as
he glanced at his own newspaper, recognized the handwriting. It
was that of Major Walsin-Esterhazy, a client with whom his bank
had many dealings; and he got in touch with Mathieu Dreyfus.
Armed with this knowledge, Mathieu Dreyfus wrote to the Minister of War and made an explicit charge. He also sent a copy of his
letter to a newspaper for publication. The General Staff was thus
driven to action, and Esterhazy had to face an inquiry. It was held
behind locked doors. The experts who had declared that the handwriting of the *bordereau* was that of Dreyfus repeated their testimony, and Esterhazy was triumphantly acquitted.

None the less, the suspicion of injustice had taken root. Many
did not believe that the General Staff acted impartially, and among
them was Georges Clemenceau. This savage-tongued patriot,
once Mayor of Montmartre, had two governing passions: hatred
of the Germans who had seized two provinces, and hatred of
the royalists at home. He had seen his father arrested by the order
of the Emperor and sent to Algeria, and he was to spend a few
weeks himself in Mazas jail. Disgusted with rule from the Tuil-
eries, he crossed the Atlantic and watched the closing phases of the
American Civil War. Experience as well as temperament made
him almost a fanatical republican, and because he believed that the
Church was in league with the royalists he warred against her
influence in the schools and, in particular, in the Army.

For the Army was not needed to defend throne and altar. It was needed for France destined to regain her provinces. As a deputy of the Assembly in Bordeaux, Clemenceau had refused to pass the Treaty of Frankfort. His contempt for all things German did not fall short of a Jewish officer with a German name, and when he first heard of Dreyfus's condemnation, he declared that the man deserved to be shot. He spoke as though he had closed his mind. Yet he was all attention when he heard that the incriminating *bordereau* had been shown to the judges, but was deliberately withheld from the prisoner and his lawyer. The verdict against Dreyfus at a secret trial, Clemenceau realized, had been secured through a breach of the law; and at once he changed his attitude. He still believed that Dreyfus was guilty; but, guilty or innocent, he was entitled to justice. Esterhazy's acquittal was a heavy blow, but Clemenceau acted quickly. He arranged that *L'Aurore* should publish an open letter to the President of the Republic. The writer was Emile Zola, the novelist. He made definite accusations and demanded to be brought to trial for his libels. For a headline to the letter Clemenceau chose 'J'Accuse!'

The Government was compelled to do as Zola wished, and his trial began in an atmosphere charged with vitriolic hatred. The hearing was not meant to be fair, for the judges ruled that no witness might suggest the innocence of a man legally condemned. Thus they crippled the witnesses for the defence, while leaving the witnesses for the prosecution free to emphasize the condemned man's guilt. Yet Clemenceau, in his defence of Zola, treated Esterhazy as the man really on trial. He put to him one searching question after another, and Esterhazy dared not answer. He knew too much. Silence damned him, and it damned the General Staff. The verdict, none the less, went against Zola, who vainly sought escape from his enemies by leaving France. He lost a case, but he had served a cause; and Clemenceau was not the only man to leave a noisy court convinced that Dreyfus was innocent.

Many officers no longer spoke to Esterhazy. The clash of loyalties grew sharper. The strain upon guilty men was becoming intolerable. They had taken a false step before, and they would take others. One day Cavaignac, as Minister of War, told the Chamber that a new document had come to light and that Dreyfus's guilt was now put beyond the reach of doubt. He reckoned without Picquart. The Calvinist had come back from Africa alive, and he refused to be silent any longer. He wrote to the Prime Minister, telling him that the new document was a forgery. He was promptly arrested, and then the guilty men took fright. Colonel Henry confessed that he had forged the new document; and in shame he cut his throat. It was now Esterhazy's turn to speak the truth, and he confessed that he was the forger of the original *bordereau*. He turned forger, he explained, at the command of the General Staff.

Stubbornly many thousands of anti-Dreyfusards resisted the exposure. Colonel Henry was a forger, Charles Maurras admitted, but 'a forger through patriotism'. The search for truth wore down each passion, each fear, each habit of mind. In the struggle to establish the innocence of an unlikeable Jew, France held up the mirror to herself. The noble jostled with the ignoble, the generous with the mean. Motives were sometimes confused and tortuous, but in the end justice was served. Once a dead Christian maid won her vindication, and now the time had come to rehabilitate a living Jew. The prisoner from Devil's Island was restored to honour and made a major. Picquart became a general.

At last the air was cleansed. The General Staff, reformed and shaken in its prestige, turned to the more serious duties of defending France against external dangers, and meanwhile Pétain, an obscure military professor, elaborated his own theories of future warfare. He knew that Clausewitz had become the master not only of the French General Staff, but of nearly all the military thinking in Europe, and he wanted the French to realize that Clausewitz might be fighting against Clausewitz; the antagonists would strike each other where they were strongest. In the last resort the success of an attack depended on the infantryman; but, as he was made of flesh and blood, he could not pierce the enemy's lines before the artillery had crippled the fire-power of the foe. In every advance, therefore, he must have full fire-protection. In the next conflict, Pétain believed, artillery would be massed against artillery, and the fighting would be a long and agonizing process. It would be a wearing down of resistance, a blunting of armaments, a war of attrition.

Here was dry doctrine encased in precise and exacting lectures, which made war geometrical and took away its glory. They had, moreover, to compete with the lectures of Colonel de Maud'huy, chief of the Infantry course, whose eloquent words often drew cheers and shouts of acclamation. Every evening he made his sons kneel down to pray that they might grow to be as brave as Bayard, and he easily persuaded his hearers to believe that war is an exaltation of the spirit. Only the more thoughtful, therefore, cared to leave Maud'huy's lecture-room for Pétain's. They were pleased when, at the end of the lecture, Pétain sometimes spoke lightly with them, and they liked the irony of his words, but in their talk with each other he was still old dry-as-dust. They called him 'Precis-le-sec'.

At times he managed to get on well with officers who, like Maud'huy, differed from him in temperament. They respected his thoroughness, his patience and his judgment, even when they were disconcerted by his reticence. To overcome his natural shyness and to know men well was a deliberate part of his preparation for war. The ordeal of attrition, as he envisaged it, demanded the closest integration of cavalry, infantry and artillery, and he detested a prevalent spirit of the clan which kept the artillery officer apart from the officer of light cavalry or a foot regiment. Tradition and etiquette were doing duty for common sense too long.

Hatred of the excluding clan meant that he was seldom, if ever, free from detractions. Bonnal's successor at the Staff College dismissed him, and he returned uncomplainingly to barracks at Quimper. The new Directorship was fortunately short-lived, and when the post went to General Maunoury, 'Precis-le-Sec' was soon recalled. Pétain re-rentered his lecture hall with added prestige. There was no one now to rebuke him because he preached the importance of good defensive weapons and fire-protection.

In 1908, when Clemenceau was Prime Minister for the first time, the Directorship of the Staff College again fell vacant. Clemenceau, who had chosen Picquart to be his Minister of War, was determined to make a sound appointment for the Staff College. Picquart consulted General Millet, his fellow-Protestant, and Millet knew that Foch longed to get back to the Staff College. He soon convinced the Minister that Foch was the man to make the teaching of war both bold and elastic.

In the way stood Clemenceau. The Prime Minister agreed that the post must go to the best officer, even though he happened to be a good Catholic; but he did not regard Foch as a good republican, and at the mention of his name he barked disapproval. Millet, hearing from Picquart that Clemenceau was obdurate, promptly sent Foch from Orleans to Paris to plead his own cause before the irascible statesman. He 'loathes people who flinch', Millet said. 'You're the same. You're both made for each other.' And though the interview was lively and inconclusive, Clemenceau promised to read the two books which Foch had written.

He was as good as his word. 'He swears not at you but by you now,' Picquart told Foch at Army manoeuvres, 'and you are his man.' There followed another tussle between Clemenceau and Foch; but it was Foch who won, and he went back in triumph to the Staff College. 'After having been thrown out through the window', he said, 'I returned through the front door.'

There could have been little doubt that Foch's two books—*Les Principes de la Guerre* and *De la Conduite de la Guerre*—appealed to Clemenceau, for he found a student of Clausewitz writing in the language of a modern Napoleon. In each book Foch emphasized the need for solid preparation and for sureness. From sureness and security an army delivered its master-strokes of successful assault; and from sureness sprang the will to conquer. Primacy belonged to the attack. 'Modern war', Foch wrote, 'knows but one argument: the tactical fact, battle. 'Certainly it was essential to have a superiority of weapon-power, and soldiers must be taught with the utmost care how to fire their guns. Yet in his writings Foch showed that he regarded each improvement in weapons as a new asset for the offensive. The defensive need for good weapons made little appeal to him.

A smaller man might have resented the defensive doctrine taught by Pétain, but, as Director of the Staff College, Foch set out to be a co-ordinator of teaching rather than a teacher himself. He wanted 'no pre-conceptions', he said. Pétain, too, had accepted misfortune without flinching and gone back to the Staff College 'by the front door'. Foch admired the thoroughness of his arguments, and soon he pressed his claim to be made a full colonel. This worthy colleague might be cautious and a pessimist, but he lacked the exaggerated gloom of Colonel Mayer, who argued that the future war would 'put face to face two human walls almost in contact, separated only by a strip of death'. This double wall, Mayer added, would be 'almost inert in spite of the will to advance on one side or the other, in spite of the attempts that will be made to push on'.

Mayer had studied the Englishman's war against the Boer only to find that few senior French officers troubled to treat that remote conflict seriously. Most of them felt contempt for an army which small bands of Boer farmers managed to cripple and disarray. The war in South Africa, like frequent skirmishes on the border of India, had nothing to teach French officers bent on the lofty mission of a national offensive. Even the old rival's navy gained little attention, and some believed that it was not worth a single French bayonet.

Foch, perhaps, shared their views. The wars which concerned him had been fought in 1866 and in 1870. The next war would be just as swift because the French intended it to be the great Clausewitzian stroke in reverse. This war of attack and rapid movement would need vast man-power as well as weapon-power, and Foch did not disdain to make a friend of Brigadier-General Henry Wilson, a talkative Irishman and francophile, who was head of the

British Staff College at Camberley. Between them they worked out a scheme to make a British Expeditionary Force the left wing of the armies fighting on a Western front. The spilled blood which Clausewitz demanded would be British as well as French.

The doctrines taught by Foch and Pétain were polarized, and their common ground was the emphasis upon sureness and security. Other men exaggerated their doctrines, it seemed, to the point of absurdity; for if Mayer wrote despondently of the 'two human walls' hurling death upon each other, a Captain Gilbert voiced the fashionable opinion that weapons were now of little importance. Foch was dismayed when his once favourite pupil, Colonel de Grandmaison, argued that the enemy must be attacked even before he has disclosed his moves. 'In the offensive,' he declared, 'imprudence is the best of safeguards', and he gained an ever-increasing ascendancy over the Staff College and the General Staff. Grandmaison preached the attack but it was the attack without a backbone of sureness.

Matters came to a head when, in 1911, the Germans sent a gunboat to Agadir. Their action, though more tactless than warlike, was a danger-signal, and the French General Staff examined afresh its plans for war. The last word ought to have rested with General Michel, who would have become the Commander-in-Chief. General Michel was almost certain that the Germans planned to invade through Belgium, and he was determined to have his troops ready to defend the Belgian frontier as well as Lorraine. He was thus virtually doubling the line of defence. Like Pétain, he thought defensively, and he was a merciless critic of the ideas expounded by Grandmaison. The forward group which Grandmaison led, however, was stronger than Michel realized. He planned, they told him, as though the Germans, not the French, intended to make the smashing attack. Such a fault, pardoned in an inconspicuous professor like Colonel Pétain, was inexcusable in a future Commander-in-Chief; and when General Michel heard his arguments rejected, he resigned from the War Council.

In his place the Ministry of War chose the slow-witted General

Joffre, whose laurels had been won in Madagascar. It was playing for safety, and meanwhile the forward group worked behind the scenes. 'The French Army,' Joffre announced, 'returning to its traditions, no longer knows any other law than the offensive. . . . All attacks are to be pushed to the extreme with the firm resolution to charge the enemy with the bayonets in order to destroy him. This result can only be obtained at the price of bloody sacrifices. Any other conceptions ought to be rejected as contrary to the very nature of war.' Joffre's words were really Grandmaison's.

Agadir brought changes to the Staff College. Foch left it for a command at Chaumont, and Pétain went to Arras to command the 33rd Infantry Division. Except for a course of lectures at the School of Cavalry in Saumur, his teaching days were over. He was content to give the closing years of his career to the welfare of a foot regiment and to make sure that its younger officers understood the nature of the inevitable war. He was constantly urging them to know and to understand their men, and as he entered the late fifties he became markedly paternal in his manner. Though a lonely bachelor, he liked to emphasize his belief that the good home makes a good soldier, and he gave his officers frequent leaves to visit their own homes. If they slightly over-stepped their leave he punished them, and sometimes he wrote to a parent asking for his co-operation, so that the offence might not be repeated.

Early in 1914 he heard that he was to have the temporary command of a brigade in St Omer, and he was delighted. 'There's no doubt,' he told a friend, 'I shall end as a brigadier-general, perhaps even as a Commander of the Legion of Honour. The little schoolboy at St Bertin's never expected to have such a grand career.' He rode on horseback through the market-place of St Omer and into the narrow street, where, as a schoolboy before the war, he had seen the prancing troop of Light Horse. He was himself a well-groomed officer. He kept the figure of a man still in his thirties, and the way in which he carried his lithe body added a few deceptive inches to his stature.

Yet there was no escape from the weight of years. Pétain seemed bound, in the very near future, to become an officer retired on half-pay, and near the outskirts of St Omer he found the modest house in which he meant to spend the evening of his life. Thus would end a career hard-working, honourable and dutiful. The temporary brigadier was too old and too wise to care that he had run his course well below the levels of recorded history.

He had never taken part in a campaign nor seen a skirmish. He drew his lessons from manoeuvres and from hard calculation, and he had no sure means of telling whether his doctrine of defensive warfare took root in the inquisitive minds of younger men. Yet an unpopular and awkward-mannered cadet at St Cyr had been fascinated by his lectures. The cadet was tall and angular, and his classmates called him the 'tall asparagus'. From his father, teacher in a Jesuit college in Paris, he inherited a fine intellect, and he succeeded so well at St Cyr that he earned the right to choose his future regiment. He chose the 33rd Infantry Regiment because its commanding officer was Colonel Pétain.

The 'tall asparagus' was Charles de Gaulle.

CHAPTER TWO

ATTRITION

THE temporary brigadier began training his men for the next manoeuvres, and the sweep of events which followed the murder of the Archduke Francis Ferdinand in Sarajevo took him by surprise. 'I never had a chance', he complained, 'to get my brigade in hand.' Surprise was almost everywhere the dominant emotion. Most Ministers in Paris wanted peace, and Louis Barthou, the Prime Minister, said to the German Ambassador: 'Give us back Alsace-Lorraine, and we shall be the best of friends.' The Tsar did not want a general war, nor did the Kaiser. Even when Germany's war with Russia was becoming a certainty, the Kaiser imagined that it need not involve France. The younger Moltke told him bluntly that he was wrong. Millions of soldiers, he said, were ready for a two-front war, and all the work of preparation could not now be undone. 'Your uncle', the Kaiser replied, 'would have given me a different answer.'

Military theorists, unknown to civilians and little-known even to soldiers, came into their own to treat the human millions as the pawns of a bewildering game. Yet, in Germany or France, only a handful of generals had been under actual fire. They had been reared as commanders on paper plans and manoeuvres and, like the statesmen whom they despised, they did not know what would happen when Clausewitz the Teuton met Clausewitz the Gaul.

The Germans went promptly to the aid of the avenging Austrians. They demanded that the French should declare their neutrality within eighteen hours and, as a pledge, they were to hand over the fortresses of Toul and Verdun. There came a reverberating echo of the September morning when revolutionary Paris heard that the Prussians had captured Verdun, and when the tocsin rang out to summon the citizens to arms. For Verdun is a gateway to Paris, and the demand for its occupation was an act of war. Roused to implacable anger, the French faced yet again the old invader.

For a second time officers drank to the day when they should meet each other in Berlin. The Germans, as General Michel had foretold, invaded Belgium, and soon Pétain was at the head of his brigade marching into the Ardennes. Many of the men were bitterly disappointed when he halted them before they neared the music of the guns, for they were afraid of losing their chance to become front-line fighters. Their awakening was rude and swift, for when Pétain moved forward again it was to defend a sector of the Meuse to the south of Dinant. The enemy had already begun his assault on Dinant, and the men saw the first of many pitiable processions of the old, the infirm and the very young escaping from their unsheltered homes.

Two days later they were facing the enemy themselves, and as soon as the firing began Pétain hurried to tell the officer in command of the artillery to train his guns right on the foe's emplacements. He brushed aside the excuse that the nature of the ground, which was cavernous and heavily wooded, forbade accurate firing. An artilleryman, he said sternly, must use his wits; otherwise he could not hope to give proper protection to the infantryman. Under fire—and it was his own baptism—Pétain cared nothing for peace-time etiquette, and while making himself a terror to the artillerymen, he was just as exacting with the infantrymen, whom he put to all kinds of unexpected tasks. The troops who relieved them were amazed to find trenches neatly dug, barricades erected and barbed wire strung from post to post. These makeshift fortifications looked starkly defensive and unheroic.

Nor could they prevent a retreat. Almost every day there came a new order to withdraw. The fighting lasted for nearly a month

before the brigade got its first chance to attack, and then it drove
the enemy out of the woods which encircled a farm at Bertaigne-
ment. Soldiers reached the blazing farmhouse only to be driven
back by fierce and overwhelming German fire, and night, when it
fell, was made hideous with the groans of wounded men. Pétain
called for doctors and for stretcher-bearers, and before they were
found there came again the order for an immediate withdrawal.
Retreat seemed to be unending, and amid the general confusion
no member of the brigade knew how the war was shaping.

Throughout each withdrawal Pétain walked behind his men, so
that he might keep a backward glance at the enemy's position. He
could also judge the spirit of his men and spot those no longer
fitted for the struggle. At one time the brigade was completely
isolated and then Pétain marched it southwards until it reached
Morceau-le-Neuf. Though the village was already crowded with
straggling and footsore soldiers, a small room was found for the
brigade commander, and he had his first night of unbroken sleep
for nearly a fortnight. He awoke to be told that he was now a
general and that he must take command of the Sixth Division.

General Pétain went to a market-place, where he could see some
of his new troops marching past. Their ranks were broken; their
backs, still fantastically burdened with equipment, were no longer
soldierly; their step as they marched was heavy. Each turned his
eyes to the chief whom he did not know, and they were eyes in
which the glamour of war was spent. Pétain did not speak, but he
understood. The will to conquer had vainly pitted the flesh, blood
and nerves of mortal men against the machine. No reality of war
was harsher than the firing of the guns or the unceasing whizz of
bullets aimed at soldiers of France conspicuously clad in blue
tunics and red trousers.

One day's retreating march wearily followed another. Pétain
insisted that the marching should be well-disciplined, and he
stormed at its commanding officer when a cavalry division in
double column stepped between his main infantry and the artillery. Once he was forced to wait because the division which pre-

ceded his own got on to the road two hours late. In an effort to
make up lost time, he ordered the infantrymen to march in single
column on each side of the road, and his innovation left the middle
of the road clear for the passage of artillery and convoy
wagons.

Time was precious, for when Pétain reached his headquarters
at Louau in the evening, he received an unexpected message: 'Tomorrow we attack towards the North.' A few hours later the new
general heard the fuller details, and he was ready. The minute care
which he had given to the forced marches he now directed on the
attack. On the morning of September 6 he had his troops waiting
to advance to the south of the two villages of St Bon and Villou-
ette, and he placed his artillery where it could best give them fire-
power. At nine o'clock the Germans began a fierce cannonade,
and for a moment his men seemed to waver. But Pétain, seated on
a white horse, rode forward with a group of cavalry officers. All
could see him, and his example brought back courage. It was
almost the last touch of warfare on the 1870 pattern, and it came
from a general with the mind of a master-mechanic.

That day marked the opening of the strange battle of the Marne.
The Germans meant to win a speedy victory by striking through
Belgium, while the French meant to win theirs by plunging
through Lorraine to the Rhine. Count von Schlieffen, former
chief of the German General Staff, knew how to defeat France, and
he planned an invasion through Belgium because French Lorraine
was ringed with fortresses. He decided that the left wing of a
German army facing French Lorraine should be modest in weight
and size, while a massive right wing should be ready to swing
through Belgium and Northern France. This right wing was not
to aim at Paris. It was to cross the Seine near Rouen and to swing
well behind Paris and her suburbs. No less than fifty-three divisions were to be used for the swinging right wing, while the static
left wing needed only seven divisions. If the French chose to drive
the left wing back to the Rhine, they would inflict little damage;
for the more they pushed back the left wing, the more swiftly

would the right wing swing to trap them and to deny them space for manoeuvre. It was the plan of the swing-door.

'It must come to a fight,' Schlieffen said as he lay dying. 'Only make the right wing strong.' But the younger Moltke, who succeeded him, lacked his courage. He begun bolstering up the left wing at the expense of the right. He left seven of his right wing divisions behind in Belgium and then, through fear of Russia, he diverted another four to East Prussia. Early in September he allowed von Kluck, the first Army Commander, to sweep inwards, instead of round the west side of Paris. It was a fatal change in the Schlieffen plan and General Gallieni, realizing in time what Kluck set out to do, urged Joffre and the British to launch a counter-attack without any delay.

Daily marches of twenty miles or more along dusty roads and under a scorching sun exhausted the Germans almost as much as the retreating French. They lost touch with their food supplies, and once Moltke gave up the Schlieffen plan he was at a loss to put another in its place. For all their courage and discipline, the Germans were the slaves of bureaucratic methods. They did not know the collective mind of the Supreme Command, which they had left far behind in Luxembourg. In the moment of French assault and German indecision the war changed its character. Propagandists called the battle of the Marne a decisive victory.

So it was. But the price of victory was terrible. Rapid movement gave place to attrition. Clausewitz, though frustrated on the fields of battle, had schooled the generals of many nations to take for granted the brutal draughts of blood-spilling. The dragon, as it fed voraciously on human flesh, clutched the innocent-seeming youth of Britain. On the eve of war only a few of Asquith's colleagues in the Cabinet realized that the scheme which Foch worked out with Henry Wilson committed them to sending a large expeditionary force across the Channel. The rest assumed that war, if it came, meant blockade, naval battles, and sharp raids on the Continent. The Foch-Wilson scheme had to go forward because no other had been devised to take its place; and now there was no retreat for the British soldiers from their fateful position as the left wing of the agonized armies fighting in France. The people who loved careless freedom saw that they must soon submit to the Continental scourge of military conscription and that the Channel would mark a perpetual crossing to mutilation and to death. Youth must keep company with rotting corpses. The mask was torn from civilization.

The disillusioning weeks ruined many military reputations, but Pétain had been proved right. He had been sagacious in retreat and bold in attack. 'Imagination, will-power, technical skill and knowledge: this is the order of the three qualities which a commander ought to have.' So Pétain argued, and he was certainly a resourceful technician. With each new danger, moreover, he seemed to grow in mental and moral stature, and less than two months after taking command of the Sixth Division he rose to be commander of the 33rd Army Corps. He reached Arras at an unquiet hour. The Germans, entrenched less than a mile from the suburbs of the great arterial city, had begun to recover from the shock of the Marne battle. But immediately, and almost silently, the 'machine-minder' general put its defences into better order.

He had come suddenly to influence, and he used it to impress upon other generals the extreme urgency of ample munitions. The battle of the Marne, he told them, did not win back the lost ironworks and factories of the North, and Germany's new hold upon the industrial areas must swiftly bring a crisis in arms' production. Outwardly the generals agreed with him, but Pétain knew that they were still 'attack-minded'. They relied too much upon manpower, which seemed to them inexhaustible, and too little upon fire-power; and France might fritter away the valour of her troops through a shortage of shells. He was, in fact, in Arras for less than a month when he received an order limiting him to a supply of four hundred shells, which he had to ration between the three divisions of his Army Corps; and the front which they held was about twenty kilometres long.

Yet only three days later Foch, now commander of the North-

ern Armies, was talking eagerly of an attack designed to pierce the
enemy's lines. Though he had lost a son in the dark days of the
retreat, nothing seemed to daunt his offensive spirit. With an
extravagant wave of the arm he threw out ideas, and at his side
was Colonel Maxime Weygand—energetic, slight, impeccably
efficient—ready to translate them, if need be, into immediate
action. The shortage of shells, the relentless approach of winter
did not trouble him. The spirit knew how to surmount the stark
geography of attrition.

Sometimes Foch had to listen with impatience to British plans
for a diversion through the Dardanelles, and, like Joffre, he
scorned a proposal from Winston Churchill, an English politician barely forty years old, that there should be a combined naval
and military assault on the Belgian coast. The Western front, Foch
insisted, was the front of decision, and no matter how heavy the
armour-plating of the German armies might become, French
valour would know how to pierce it; and in 1915 there began careful preparations for a major attack in the early summer. Its main
objective was Vimy Ridge, a line of hills about five miles to the
north-east of Arras, and Pétain's Army Corps was to bear the
chief burden of the attack. As commander of the attacking Tenth
Army, General d'Urbal summoned Pétain and his other army
corps and divisional commanders to a conference. He asked each
to state the number of grenades which he would need. 'Five thousand,' the most ambitious had said. Then came Pétain's turn to
answer. 'I want fifty thousand.' The reply astonished d'Urbal, but
the commanders who followed Pétain gave the same answer. As
the day approached President Poincaré visited the front chosen
for the attack. With him was Sir Henry Wilson, and in his diary
he described their meeting with Pétain, 'a tall, strapping, beauti-
fully groomed soldier, who explained with luminous clarity his
arrangements and dispositions, but had no illusions as to any blazing success'.

Though his fears were well-founded, Pétain could hardly complain that his own troops were unprepared. He had visited each

battery in turn, and he had made each fire a round so that the men might know the targets which were fixed in his artillery plan. Not a single corporal escaped his questioning. Three miles ahead of his men lay the crest of Vimy Ridge, and on May 9 there began a savage cannonade: 'twelve hundred guns served by Frenchmen,' wrote Wilson in his diary, 'and lashing to their utmost. No living person has ever before heard or seen such a thing.' The guns stopped their firing, and the French swept on for two and a half miles almost without hindrance. Some actually reached the crest of the ridge. They took the Germans so completely by surprise that for a moment the Crown Prince Rupprecht of Bavaria thought of moving his Army Group headquarters away from Lille. But the French in their turn were surprised; and, in spite of his reputation for thinking of everything, Pétain had kept only a brigade in corps reserve. His generalship was thorough, but it lacked genius. He had bent his mind to a limited aim, and the moment which only genuis or supreme audacity might have seized was lost. The Germans hurried to close the gap, and within six days thirteen enemy divisions faced the struggling 10th Army.

Despite this re-assertion of German strength, Foch ordered a general advance. It lasted two days, served no purpose and cost the French more than 100,000 casualties. The High Command softened the blow by claiming that decisive victory at this battle of Artois had been missed by a narrow margin, but Pétain refused to accept this view. On the contrary, he argued, the whole operation showed the folly of 'starting an offensive without sufficiently consulting those who have to carry it out'; and when Poincaré paid another visit to Arras a corps commander begged him, as President of the Republic, to put a stop to local offensives. 'The instrument of victory', he said, 'is being broken in our hands.'

Joffre's reply was to plan for the autumn a two-pronged offensive. The British were to assist the French in a new attack on Artois and, almost simultaneously, the French were to launch an attack in Champagne. Once more the main burden of the attack in Artois was to fall on the 10th Army; but now Pétain had risen to the command of the 2nd Army, which was selected to lead the attack in Champagne. As the summer weeks advanced Joffre decided that the attack in Champagne was more important than the attack in Artois, and he pinned his faith on Pétain's leadership.

But Pétain was not his own master. The 2nd Army formed part of an army group which included the 4th Army under General Langle de Cary, and the group commander was General Castelnau. He had to work in harmony with them. He was given 27 divisions for his main attack on a twelve-kilometres' front to the east of Rheims. He was also given 850 heavy guns, whereas Foch and Douglas Haig between them had only 534 heavy guns; and he won from Castelnau and Langle de Cary an explicit agreement that unless they smashed the German front at their first blow they must regard the attack as a failure.

On September 25 the attack was launched in Champage. The troops broke through the enemy's first position and, on the following day, they reached the second position only to find that there the Germans had skilfully placed their main artillery. Pétain, realizing what had happened, was anxious to admit the failure of the attack, but, in the heat of the battle, his colleagues forgot their agreement. Castelnau over-ruled him, and the heavy fighting lasted for another three days. The whole offensive took a toll of a quarter-million Allied casualties, of whom 143,000 were Frenchmen under Castelnau's command.

The slaughter sobered the judgment alike of rulers and soldiers, and before the year ended Foch was using language which echoed Pétain's. 'It is a fact', he wrote, 'that the infantry attack always halts and fails at that point where the preparation has not been sufficient. Once more we see that the power of organization is stronger than the bravery of the troops.' Early in the New Year he described the right method of attack as 'a series of successive acts, each necessitating a great quantity of artillery and very little infantry'. Meanwhile Pétain, who must have agreed with every word that Foch was now writing, had left the field for headquarters at Noailles. He was to take four army corps behind the lines under his wing, re-plan their military training and prepare them for the interminable war of attrition. Fate seemed determined to give him renown as the educator of an army.

Events on the scorched front, however, persistently challenged men's judgments and reputations. Joffre, Foch and Haig had chosen the Somme for their next offensive. The Germans, they imagined, were too busy humiliating the Russians to trouble about a major offensive of their own in the West, and Joffre dismissed the earlier reports that they had begun to mass for an attack on Verdun. Such an attack, his staff assured him, could only be a diversion. They forgot that the Chief of the German General Staff thought as a German, and not as a Frenchman.

General von Falkenhayn, who succeeded the younger Moltke, had watched the German armies as they advanced beyond Brest Litovsk without breaking the resistance of the Russians, and he worried over the ever-lengthening lines of his communications in the East. He wanted the military decision to be reached in the West. Paris was a nearer and a greater goal than St Petersburg or Moscow. The gateway was still Verdun. Beyond it stretched the road to Paris, and that glittering prize, once taken, would bring the war with France to an end. The British, perhaps, would sooner beg for peace than allow their troops to be hurled back to the Channel.

The Kaiser went to Mezières to see some of the massive work of preparation, and the army chosen for the honour of smashing a way through the defences of Verdun had for its ostensible commander the Crown Prince Wilhelm. More imperishable glory was about to encompass the House of Hohenzollern. The approaching battle, so Army Orders told the German soldier, was 'the last offensive against the French'.

No matter how staff officers in Chantilly interpreted German intentions, it was scarcely possible to deceive the soldiers who endured a biting winter in the hills and wooded valleys on either side of the Meuse as it flowed northwards from Verdun. Even the silence which sometimes fell over the German trenches seemed to them heavy and ominous. General Sarrail, who commanded at

Verdun in the earlier months of the war, believed that the neighbourhood was bound to become the theatre of a decisive battle. Whenever possible, he had engaged in local attacks, so that he might push back the German lines and allow more room for manoeuvre to soldiers who must one day defend important outposts of the Verdun fortifications—like the hill of Mort Homme on the left bank of the Meuse, or the forts of Douaumont and Vaux on the right.

The sense of expectancy gripped nearly all the troops within the Verdun saliant. In the bewildering first weeks of the war many had marched twenty miles or more a day but, now that the front was static, they showed once more the tenacity of a people tied to the land. They hated to see a single acre of France churned into unprofitable mud. They stood between the foe and the farmstead. 'They shall not pass': the legendary words may have been uttered for the first time long before the early morning of February 21, 1916, when the storm broke with a fury never before experienced on any field of battle.

Never before, in fact, had so much artillery been massed for an attack. The light turned ashen-grey with smoke, dust and the trail of gas shells. The noise deafened men, so that they could not hear each other speak. Large trees, uprooted by the bursting of heavy shells, went hurtling through the air. Within an hour almost all the front-line trenches were obliterated. All telephonic lines were cut, and the barbed-wire entanglements which the French fashioned carefully for their defence were blown away. Men climbed into new craters and shell-holes, where they waited for the bombardment to die down or to stop as abruptly as it had begun. But it was to last for more than ten hours, and when the lull came survivors nerved themselves for the inevitable onrush of German foot-soldiers.

Wave after wave of infantry poured into the desolated area that had been the Haumont wood, and amid hundreds of dying men they found defenders fighting until their last bullets was spent. Next day the Germans concentrated their withering fire on the nearby Caures wood, which was being held by two battalions of Light Infantry. Their commander was Colonel Driant, a politician and deputy for the city of Nancy. When he saw the first wave of German infantry advancing he shouted to the men in the first trench: 'Charge, my children. Long live France!' Before the evening he knew that the position of his two battalions was hopeless, for the Caures wood was almost surrounded. 'In a few minutes', he told his staff, 'we shall have to meet death or become prisoners; but, perhaps, we can save some of these brave lads.' Then he told the survivors what to do. They were to destroy everything which they could not carry away, and when this was done, they were to separate into five columns and try to escape. Many, as they left the wood, were mown down by machine-gun fire. Driant was the last to retire, and within the wood he was killed.

The French often fought like demons, even when their communications were cut and no food could reach them. Sometimes they gave up their drinking water to cool the guns; but the sheer weight of metal and numbers drove them back, and when they were no longer able to cling to the dismantled fort at Douaumont, the citadel of Verdun lay in immediate peril. Out-gunned and out-manned, the French had to summon to their aid a moral weapon. It was not the vaunted will to conquer; it was the steely determination to defend the soil of France and to resist. Nerve had to prolong the uneven fight with metal. 'They shall not pass'; and soon after Douaumont had fallen, a new commander arrived at the troubled salient. For, on the night of February 24, the reports which reached Chantilly were so startling that Castelnau roused Joffre from his sleep. Joffre agreed that something must be done, and done at once. He was ready to give full powers to Castelnau. Then he thought of Pétain, whom he summoned from the training ground. He gave him the task of defending Verdun, and at the end of his talk he said: 'Well, my friend, now you are easy in your mind.'

Many days went by before Pétain became easy in his mind. No sooner had he entered his new headquarters at Souilly than he

gave brief orders to the commanders on both sides of the Meuse.
They must hold on; they must not yield. Yet he knew that withdrawal was a certainty unless many more guns and men were
brought to the relief of the defences before Verdun. The railway
line from Paris came directly under German fire. The road from
Bar-le-Duc, therefore, must take its place; and, with a few peremptory demands, Pétain turned it into a military highway. He
had it equipped with 175 repair stations and with many petrol
pumps and water tanks, and he summoned all the available taxi-
cabs of Paris to serve as troop-carriers. He allowed nothing to
obstruct the road, and every car or wagon which had engine-
trouble was soon pushed towards the ditch. Within a week of his
arrival the road from Bar-le-Duc had carried 190,000 men as well
as 23,000 tons of munitions. The speed with which a machine-
minded general augmented his artillery and brought fresh troops
to the battlefield surprised the enemy. To pierce the defences of
Verdun was a harder task than any senior officer close to the
Crown Prince had imagined.

The Germans, none the less, still took pride in the better
quality and far greater number of their own guns. They realized
that the French would seek to ease the pressure on Verdun by
launching an offensive elsewhere; and the more the plans for this
offensive took shape, the more eager became the Germans to
reach a decision on the Meuse. Pétain himself kept a watchful eye
on preparations for a Somme offensive, and without it the battle
of Verdun would have been lost. Yet ceaselessly he asked for more
divisions and for more artillery, well knowing that each demand
made a new drain on the men and equipment needed for the
Somme offensive. Inevitably the hammer-blows at Verdun were
to change the scope of the offensive and to throw on the British
an ever-increasing burden of the attack.

For Pétain insisted that the men who had to endure the furnace
of Verdun must be continuously relieved; and he asked for a
'chain-pump' of reserves and fresh divisions. Otherwise the ordeal
would become more than flesh and blood could stand. Metal

would destroy nerve, and Verdun must fall. The succour of fresh divisions brought the angels of death to almost every village in France, and many a sunlit street was made mournful by the sight of a mother or young woman garbed as a widow.

Half the army, it seemed, was passing through the crucible on the Meuse; and if any man deserved to be called the 'saviour' of Verdun, it was the common soldier, anonymous and bitter-tongued. Pétain was the apex of a nerve-tormented pyramid. He found, already formed, a titanic will to defend; and for leadership he brought technical knowledge, cold calculation, a kinsman's sympathy with the peasant turned soldier, and a long patience. He became a symbol of the soldiers' endurance just because he was neither eloquent nor romantic. His task, like theirs, was to hang on. All his adult life he had scorned caste-distinctions and the loyalties of a clan. Now his thoughts were on the human strain of battle, and he fell into a fine rage when he found that a large rest-camp for his troops had been placed within sound of the guns. Temperament made him a pessimist, and he refused to disguise from Joffre or from any Minister the extreme gravity of the situation. The Somme offensive, however much his demands weakened its nature, was imperative. The battle of Verdun was a battle against time.

France, however, was perpetually at odds with herself. The will to defend still conflicted with the urge to attack, and though soldiers in their tens of thousands had died on the heights of the Meuse to prevent skilful and courageous Germans from piercing the defences of Verdun, the belief persisted that the German defences in their turn could be pierced. Pétain was haunted by the fear that at any moment Joffre might make a radical change of plan. After the battle had raged for more than nine weeks Pétain was made a Grand Officer of the Legion of Honour. The commendation was flattering, but he had reason to distrust those who brought him gifts; for on the same day Joffre ordered him to begin preparations for taking Fort Douaumont. A week later he was given the command of the central group of armies, and General Nivelle took his place as the officer immediately responsible for the defence of Verdun. With dark foreboding Pétain took the superior command, and under compulsion he gave Nivelle freedom of action just when the Germans were about to make their attack more intensive and when the bow of defence was tautened almost to breaking point.

But the former college boy from St Omer was not the only little-known officer who had leaped to fame in the first months of the war. Nivelle, who commanded the 5th Infantry Regiment at the outbreak of war, rose quickly to the command of the 3rd Army Corps. With abounding confidence he planned the recapture of Fort Douaumont. The assault was brilliant, but Pétain did not doubt that his countrymen would be driven back. Throughout the whole Verdun salient, he insisted they were still outgunned and out-manned. He despised a needless sacrifice of life, an impudent search for glory amid wasteful suffering.

Soon the Germans were thrusting against the outer defences of Verdun. They stormed Mort Homme on the left bank of the Meuse and Fort Vaux on the right. Each stronghold was bravely defended. In Fort Vaux the commander was Major Raynal, who had asked for a fortress command after receiving severe wounds in the early years of the war. He and his handful of men went on fighting, though they were almost driven mad with thirst and the Germans were surrounding the fort and throwing grenades through the broken windows. 'We are near the end,' Major Raynal told the defenders at last. 'Officers and men have done their whole duty. Long live France!' He surrendered, and the Crown Prince, moved to admiration, allowed him to keep his sword. From his German captors he heard that he had been made a commander in the Legion of Honour.

Even with the loss of the Verdun outposts, with the names of which nearly all Frenchmen were now familiar, the defensive spirit barely flagged. But Nivelle, chastened by his failure, realized that the war of attrition ruthlessly imposed its own logic, and when Poincaré went to Amiens to preside at a conference on the coming

Somme offensive, he felt bound to tell Joffre, Haig and Foch what
he had heard from Nivelle as well as from Pétain. Both had said:
'Verdun will be taken.'

The Somme offensive opened only just in time, but as soon
as Falkenhayn understood its nature he sent no more fresh divisions to the Verdun salient, which gradually ceased to be the
major theatre of war. In the autumn, therefore, Pétain invited
Nivelle to renew his attempts to take Fort Douaumont. The plan
was carried out faultlessly. Both Fort Douaumont and ruined Vaux
fell to the French; and the battle of Verdun, so the people joy-
ously believed, was over. There was no triumphal entry into Paris
now for the Crown Prince. The only solid gain for the German
effort was a battle-charred area of about twelve square miles embracing in its mud and stench a few derelict forts and hamlets. The
struggle had taken a toll of a million lives, German and French,
and it taught the thoughtful that a war of attrition knows no
victor.

Yet Nivelle's triumph brought a fleeting glamour to the detest-
able war. The battle of the Somme was soon to draw wearily to a
standstill, after causing endless frictions between the French and
British commanders and exacting nearly a million French, British
and German casualties. Were the methods of attrition really justified? Was Europe to bleed to death? In Paris Aristide Briand, a dis-
tracted Prime Minister, listened to the men who were praising
Nivelle, a new hero of Verdun and amply endowed with dash and
courage. Joffre's massive day was coming to an end. The Government made him the supreme military adviser, but he ceased actually to command the French armies on the Western front. Civilian-minded Ministers decided that the new commander must be
a general acceptable to the Chamber of Deputies, and they readily
agreed that Nivelle was far more ingratiating than Pétain. Thus
Nivelle took Joffre's place.

Once he charmed with his modesty, but now the impact of
sudden fortune laid bare his vanity and arrogance. He became
boastful and assertive. What he had done on the Verdun salient

D

he would now repeat, on a tenfold scale, along the Aisne between Soissons and Rheims. On a front forty kilometres long he would provide a massive artillery cover unprecedented in all the battles of the war, and wave after wave of infantrymen would leap forward to pierce the German lines. They would sweep beyond the tantalizing heights known as the Chemin des Dames and flood through the flat country around Laon. All would be done in a single day. That day—J-day, as Nivelle called it in his plan—would go down in history as the day when France achieved resounding victory almost without bloodshed. Proudly the new Commander-in-Chief showed the plan to Pétain.

'Precis-le-sac' was not impressed. He had invited Nivelle to counter-attack at Verdun only when he knew at last that conditions were favourable. He saw no just parallel between Verdun and the Aisne. In the Verdun salient the French knew nearly every inch of the ground taken by the Germans, but on the Aisne nature favoured the enemy, who could assume the defensive, while having many advantages over the French. The attack, Petain argued, would require exceptionally good weather; but, even so, it could not be launched without a heavy loss of life. Nivelle said nothing. He merely decided to go ahead without Pétain's advice or help.

Yet the recklessness of the Nivelle plan troubled General Hubert Lyautey, the greatest of French pro-consuls, whom Briand had summoned from Morocco to be Minister of War. Lyautey was an aristocrat and at heart a royalist. He could be as bold as Foch, whom he admired, but he knew from his own colonial warfare the necessity for careful preparation, and he despised Nivelle's boasts. When the plan was ready, Nivelle sent Colonel Georges Renouard to the rue Saint-Dominique to explain it to the Minister of War, not knowing that Renouard once worked closely with Lyautey in Southern Oran.

'Renouard,' the Minister exclaimed impatiently, 'this is a plan for the Grand Duchess of Gerolstein.'

The colonel went on explaining the Nivelle plan.

'Renouard,' Lyautey cried, 'you've got to answer me. I'm

not Minister of War now, and you're not Colonel Renouard. We're two Frenchmen face to face, and it is a question of the safety of France. What do you really think of the plan you have brought me?'

'General, I am here as General Nivelle's subordinate and messenger. I am not entitled to criticize my superior officer.'

'Come, come, my dear Georges. Look me in the eyes. Just fancy you are once again my confidential officer at Ain-Sefra and tell me the truth. What do you think of it?'

There were tears in Renouard's eyes.

'General, I think as you do. It is madness.'

To dismiss Nivelle, idol of a public thirsting for victory, seemed impossible. Lyautey found relief by going back to Morocco. His resignation led almost at once to the downfall of Briand's ministry, and his place at the rue Saint-Dominique was taken by Paul Painelevé. The new Minister had a genuine respect for Pétain's judgment, and he was just as disconcerted as Lyautey had been by the Commander-in-Chief's buoyant optimism. 'Victory is certain,' Nivelle insisted. 'The front will be ruptured without loss. The Craonne plateau is in our pocket.' And when Poincaré remarked that in the sector chosen for the attack the enemy had doubled the number of his batteries and division, Nivelle replied: 'So much the better. We shall take more prisoners.'

As it happened, the enemy was doing something far bolder and more sagacious than doubling his batteries and divisions. Instead of Falkenhayn, he now had Hindenburg and Ludendorff for his military leaders, and they had decided to wage a defensive war in the West. They knew—so talkative were Nivelle's supporters— just where the French would launch their attack. With the utmost secrecy, therefore, they drew a new Hindenburg line and, on a front of forty kilometres, they ordered the troops to withdraw from their first position and retire to their second. As they retired, they scorched the ground and covered it with booby traps. In the enemy's master-stroke Pétain saw a reflection of his own defensive methods, and now he was more than ever certain that the

French plan for attack ought to be scrapped. Nivelle dismissed his objections.

Soon all Paris seemed to be discussing J-day. A general had at last arisen to wear the mantle of Napoleon and to punish swiftly the impudent invader. The plan in nearly all its details was shown to many hundreds of officers, and the least military-minded civilians professed to know that the Aisne was to mark the theatre of final victory. Ludendorff declared it to be a red-letter day for the German Army when a copy of the plan was found on a young captain taken prisoner near Maison-de-Champagne.

The more widely the plan was known, however, the more emphatic its critics became, and when Painlevé asked once more for his views Pétain gave a careful answer. The engagement, he said, would have to begin in fair weather and after ample preparation by the artillery. With a heavy sacrifice of life the attack might pierce the first and second lines of the enemy's defences; but at the third line it would encounter the reserves which had been sheltered against the heaviest gunfire. To overcome such massive defence in the space of a few hours was a project as dangerous as it was absurd.

While the people waited impatiently for the thrust to victory, the disquiet within the Ministry of War became so grave that Poincaré decided to intervene. He entered the Presidential train, and when it reached Compiègne he held a secret conference. He was ready to hear the three army group commanders—Micheler, Franchet d'Esperey and Pétain—debating with Nivelle. But Pétain did not debate. He became cold and impassive. It was an idle dream, he said, to imagine that the French could pierce the second line of defence in one day. Even if it could be done, it required the most careful preparation and timing; and heavy losses would have to be endured for an uncertain result. Before Pétain had finished, Nivelle lost his temper. 'Since I agree neither with the Government nor with my subordinates,' he said, 'there is nothing for me to do except to hand my resignation to the President of the Republic.'

'There can be no dismissal, General, on the eve of a great battle.'

Poincaré's voice was sharp; but, as there was no dismissal, the plan went forward. The people wanted it. So did many thousands of troops who sincerely believed Nivelle when he said that victory would be certain and almost bloodless. Twice J-day was postponed, and each time there was intense irritation. The longing for titanic movement fitted the momentous events elsewhere. In March the Tsar was driven from his throne. On April 6—the very day of Poincaré's conference in the train at Compiègne—Woodrow Wilson brought the United States into the war. Three days later the British began their formidable battle of Arras. April 16 was J-day, and the three large armies on the Aisne launched their attack.

Within an hour, as the first waves of infantrymen lay tortured by the heavy German fire, it was obvious that the day of victory had not dawned. The troops who followed them saw the agony of comrades caught in the uncut wire. Many were slaughtered by their own guns as they fired short. With the utmost difficulty infantrymen reached the first German line only to find it virtually empty of troops, for the defence was massed, as their commanders knew, in the second line. No matter how hard they fought, they were beaten by the superior fire of the Germans and by the strength of the foe's defensive position. By the end of a fortnight they had taken 45,000 prisoners and 450 guns. But more than a hundred thousand Frenchmen lay dead, and when the butchering nature of the battle became known to the people a deep gloom fell over them.

Within a month of J-day Nivelle ceased to be Commander-in-Chief. Pétain took his place. He faced a task even graver than the one which had confronted him at Verdun. There was mutiny in the Army.

CHAPTER THREE

COMMANDER-IN-CHIEF

THE mutiny spread until more than half the soldiers of France were in some way affected. Its immediate begettor was the failure of the offensive. Carnage mocked Nivelle's promise that there would be little loss of life, and men waiting to relieve their comrades in the front line braced themselves for death. Many had faced the guns at Verdun, but now death seemed purposeless, and soldiers compared their bestial conditions with the easy circumstances of factory workers earning fifteen to twenty francs a day in Paris. Revolution was in the air, and French soldiers heard how troops in Russia were forming Soviet committies to decide when to go into action and whom to obey.

For that matter two Russian brigades were holding the line before Brimont. On the eve of Nivelle's offensive each company in the brigades took a vote to decide whether or not they should join in the attack. By a large majority they agreed to fight. Their courage proved to be exemplary, but French troops noted that they were not saluting their officers nor showing respect for superior rank. Pétain at once removed the Russian brigades to Neuchateau, but it was too late to destroy the germs of insubordination. Troops were now singing the Internationale, carrying the red flag and shouting: 'Down with war.'

The new Commander-in-Chief soon got the measure of the mutiny. He knew only too well how bad conditions on the Aisne had become. He had seen men nerving themselves for death once too often, and the situation was pitiable for a fighting soldier deprived of all confidence in his commander. In a lengthy report to Painlevé he emphasized not only the failure of the offensive, but also the onrush of revolutionary ideas, the contrast between life in the factory and life in the trenches, and the soldiers' bitterness over the increasing numbers of shirkers who lived in security well behind the front line. Some of the causes of the mutiny, Pétain wrote, were due to conditions at the front, and others to exterior influences: 'against the first the Commander-in-Chief is armed to some extent. He is not armed against the others, and here only the Government can act effectively'. And he criticized sharply the influence of the Press in Paris.

He had read articles, he declared, which showed little enthusiasm for the French successes. 'On the contrary—a coincidence all the more regrettable—the Press does not give up its dithyrambic eulogies on the exploits of our British allies. The English, so one reads, have an impeccable method of warfare, a superior artillery and a marvellous infantry. This theme is constantly exploited and the flattering tone is kept up untiringly.' If the journals were not praising England it was because they had turned their attention to Russia and were constantly reporting the changes within her army —'the creation of a committee of soldiers and workers in Petrograd, the creation of soldiers' committees in the regiments, the suppression of the salute to officers, the abolition of regular titles of address between superiors and subordinates'. They commented complacently on events in Russia and forgot that the French Army was facing 'the ferments of revolutionary ideas'. The control of the Press, Pétain admitted, was the Government's affair. 'Meanwhile one can recall that from the strict military point of view the Army has only one end—victory. It has only one virtue —discipline, which embraces all the others.'

To revolutionary excitement and the demoralizing influences of the Paris newspapers Pétain added a third exterior cause of mutiny: it was the incessant visits of deputies to the front. 'Not content with limiting their inquiries to the strict purpose of their mission, many of them ask general officers all sorts of questions. They provoke criticisms and recriminations against the High

Command. They even take account of secret information which their victims are sometimes weak enough to disclose to them in ignorance of the extent of their powers. They come down to corps officers, to subalterns and even to the troops, from whom they receive a blurred picture of the whole sweep of events without troubling to find out whether they are well founded.'

Complaints against journalists and deputies showed the military temper, and Pétain, when he committed them to writing, knew that they might be resented by Painlevé and other Ministers; but they formed an essential part of the picture which an honest Commander-in-Chief felt bound to paint. Without the Government's help, he believed, he would have no chance of quelling the mutiny. Behind him were irate and, perhaps, frightened generals who wanted stern and almost draconian measures of punishment. Pétain promised sternness, but he understood the causes of the mutiny better than most senior officers, and Painlevé, as he read the report, realized that the new Commander-in-Chief meant to apply the right remedies to a sudden sickness.

First had to come the punishment of the ringleaders, and, with his mind made up, Pétain went to a War Council summoned by Poincaré. He looked pale, but majestic. 'The evil is deep-seated,' he said, 'but it is not beyond remedy. I hope to overcome it within a few weeks. But we must make examples in the regiments which have mutinied and give up the right of pardon for those sentenced to death for any case of collective disobedience and concerted abandonment of posts.' In other words, he asked the President and the Ministers to renounce their rights of clemency. There must be no appeal, he said, from a military court. Poincaré hated the demand, but Pétain was adamant. Almost in despair the President asked that there should be as few summary executions as possible. He did not know that he was actually voicing the mind of the Commander-in-Chief. Pétain was not going to butcher his own men to appease the anger of an officer-caste. He wanted the powers of life and death vested in himself as Commander-in-Chief, so that they might be used sparingly.

The Ministers at the War Council promised to ask the Assembly for the necessary changes in military law. They were bowing, they believed, to grim necessity. As though to relieve the tension, Poincaré suddenly asked Pétain what he thought about the International Congress in Stockholm, for it was to be attended by Socialists from belligerent as well as neutral countries. 'If French delegates', he said, 'meet with German to discuss the conditions of peace, could you keep your Army under control? Could you make sure it would continue to fight?' Pétain replied firmly, 'No.'

'But,' Painlevé broke in, 'if we refuse to be represented at Stockholm we may have to face the inertia of the Russian army. Then seventy-five German divisions would be freed for action on our front.'

'Yes,' Pétain admitted. 'But the danger of seventy-five divisions freed to attack us is less grave than the complete demoralization of our Army.'

Almost the first soldier to be sentenced to death was the eighteen-year-old Corporal Léfèbre. He came from a village in Northern France which the Germans had over-run, and he saw them shooting his father and his sister as suspected spies. Amid great dangers he crossed the lines, and his gallantry soon earned him a corporal's stripes. Unhappily, he was an active mutineer, and a comrade wrenched from his hands the rifle which he was raising at his captain. Many could have witnessed against him, and Pétain ratified the death sentence. The ageing bachelor knew that the condemned youth came from his own part of France and probably belonged to the same stock as himself and his great-uncle, the Abbé Léfèbre; but he allowed nothing to stand in the way of his duty. In the middle of the night, a few hours before the lad was due to face the firing squad, Painlevé roused Pétain from his sleep to plead eloquently for a reprieve. It was useless.

Meanwhile military judges were amazed by the attitude of a convinced anti-militarist and syndicalist. The man declared that he often heard the speeches of Albert Thomas, the Socialist who had become a Minister. In the earlier speeches of his career Thomas urged listeners to disobey their military officers. 'Today,' the mutineer said, 'Albert Thomas is a Minister, and yet you condemn me to be shot. I don't understand. This disgusts me so much that I am anxious to be finished with it all.' A cogent excuse did not save him, and he went to his execution with disdainful indifference.

One afternoon a regiment stationed in Coeuvres, a village in Picardy, watched passing lorries from which men shouted: 'Down with war!' 'Down with the Army!' 'Throw away your rifles!' In the evening, while the regiment assembled for a return to the trenches, four hundred men left the ranks and, marching in good order, made for the Villers-Cotterets wood. There, in Soviet fashion, they elected their own chiefs and posted guards round the wood. They remained within the wood for four days and nights; sleeping in the open, drinking from a brook and concocting vegetable soups. On the fifth day, when hunger oppressed them, they took a vote and agreed to return to the regiment. Marching as a column and in perfect step, they left the wood. Smartness, silence and discipline gave the astonishing impression that they were a model group of soldiers.

Their mutiny, however, made it necessary to call off an attack. They were sent to a prisoners' camp, and after an inquiry most of them were transferred to a camp in North Africa. Thirty-two were left to face a court martial in Soissons, and their four days' trial became an exciting affair. The president of the court voted for thirty-two death sentences. The other judges did not wish to be so severe, but as the men had acted with disciplined unanimity, it was hard to discover the ringleaders.

Suddenly one of the accused soldiers stood up and said: 'Since you tell us that we must pay the death penalty, I offer to pay it myself for the sake of all my comrades.' The number of death sentences was reduced to seventeen. Then Poincaré pleaded with Pétain, who, moved by the conduct of the mutineers of Coeuvres, agreed that one man alone should die. The victim was not the soldier who offered his own life, but one whose previous record had been ugly and who was without a family.

Disciplined defiance was, in fact, a pronounced feature of the mutiny, and from the front-line came no weakening. 'In the front-line,' the men said, 'we will hold firm. The Boche shall not pass. But we do not want a new offensive.' They made their own distinction between mutiny and treachery. No one was going over to the enemy. Ludendorff had no idea of the calamity which befell the French Army, and when at last reports reached him it was too late. Morale had already recovered, and for the rest of his days Ludendorff regarded his ignorance of the mutiny as marking one of the lost opportunities of the war. The way in which Pétain overcame the mutiny, he wrote, was 'more important than a great victory'.

In the complaints of the mutineers Pétain heard an echo of his own views—'They shall not pass'—but he shared his countrymen's detestation of waste in human life. It was not a general's business to make out an expensive butchers' bill. Even the lives of malefactors must be taken sparingly, and though Pétain had frightened Poincaré by demanding the withdrawal of the rights of clemency and pardon, he ratified no more than twenty-six death sentences. The number of executions, moreover, was not twenty-six, but twenty-five; for Corporal Moulin owed a sudden freedom to enemy action. He was led to a field near Maizy with two other mutineers. The two men were shot, and before it came to Moulin's turn a German shell exploded in the field. Two soldiers guarding him were killed outright. In the confusion Moulin dived into a thicket and could not be found. Twenty years later he was reported to be living quietly in South America.

Once he had imposed his punishments Pétain turned swiftly to the remedies. An obvious cause of bitterness was the artificial distinction between officer and man. Rank, Pétain agreed, was necessary for discipline, but the ordinary soldier had his rights and his temperament. It was a young captain's duty to hear the complaints of his men and, when they were justified, to make a prompt report to his superiors. Too often a captain was indifferent to those beneath him in rank and anxious merely to make a good impression on his commanding officer. There were also some stiff social barriers between one set of officers and another. Snobberies and regimental rivalries stood in the way of harmonious effort, and untold harm sprang from the fighting man's dislike of the staff officer. The officer of the trench and the officer of the château lived in different worlds. Pétain brought them together as often as possible to discuss their common problems, and, above all, to consider the morale and the welfare of the men in the trenches. A fuller consideration, he was certain, could have prevented the mutiny.

Arrears of home leave created a gnawing grievance. All leave had long been stopped on the sectors of the front chosen for Nivelle's offensive, while on quieter sectors, where leave was still permitted, a youth was often given priority over the family man. Pétain made all periods of leave regular; they were to be rights, not graces. He installed wash-houses and canteens well behind the lines and thus enabled the soldiers to travel homewards clean and refreshed. The war had made railway services slow and difficult, and a man might lose two whole days of his leave before he reached his family. Pétain organized lorry transport from the front to main line stations. He issued special time-tables, so that the soldier might not be misled by faulty information. As soon as he heard that street harpies assembled in large numbers outside the terminus stations and that there was often excessive drunkenness, he put the capital out of bounds for all troops whose families did not live in Paris. He felt a special sympathy with those soldiers whose homes, like his own, were in the occupied or devastated areas, and he appealed to many ladies of France to act as godmothers to these homeless men and to invite them to their own fireside.

Nothing seemed too small for his methodical mind. He heard complaints freely, and when someone showed him a loaf of bread poor in quality, he summoned the Army quartermaster. 'This is your affair,' he said. 'See that nothing like this is produced again.' At all times, when things went wrong, he sent for the officer ultimately responsible.

He approved a new ribbon for bravery, and he liked to decorate the men himself. One day he was about to pin the new ribbon on an old soldier who bore already the red and green ribbon, to which five palms were attached.

'Five palms all to yourself! How did you get them?'

'General, I only did what everyone else has done.'

'What everyone else has done! Do you hear that?' Pétain cried, and taking the badge of the Legion of Honour from a nearby officer, he pinned it on the old soldier, whose eyes filled with tears.

As a pioneer in welfare work for an army at war, Pétain began a task which might have consumed all his energies, but the rehabilitation of the soldiers' spirit was only one of the major tasks which fell to the Commander-in-Chief. Painlevé had not been content with dismissing Nivelle. He brought back Foch, who had fallen out of favour with Joffre, and made him Chief of the General Staff. He believed that the two generals made a good pair: the one quick-witted and intuitive, the other massive in his powers of calculation. Pétain welcomed Foch's new appointment, for he admired his brilliance in the field of battle. He also knew that Foch's manners, though often excessively exuberant, were more helpful than his own in difficult dealings with the British commanders.

For, even without the mutiny, Pétain and Foch would have agreed to make 1917 a waiting year, since Nivelle's failure had been nothing less than a military disaster. Now, as in the days of the battle of the Somme, the British had to shoulder the main burden of the fighting, and in vain Sir Henry Wilson complained of the 'Pétain school of squatting and doing nothing'. A whole year must pass before the French could renew the offensive, and by that time they would have American troops at their side; the problem of man-power would be solved. Meanwhile they must pile up their armaments, and, amid the distractions of mutiny, Pétain worked out his demands for munitions. He called for more aircraft, more artillery, more gas shells; and, in the teeth of opposition from the General Staff, he gave an order for three thousand light tanks. In June General Pershing, the American commander, reached Paris, where Painlevé told him how many soldiers Pétain and Foch wished him to send within a year. They asked for a million, and Pershing sent a cable which the chiefs of the War Department in Washington read with astonishment. Like the British before them, the Americans had entered the war without realizing that France and Flanders might be the graveyards of their youth.

In this waiting year Pétain turned once more to the problems of training. He had been the prophet of attrition; but now he believed that when a million American soldiers landed in France the war would change its character. Men who had fought so long in trenches must prepare their minds for the day when they might have to fight the enemy on open ground. Methodically the Commander-in-Chief worked out his plan for incorporating the American troops within the framework of the French Army. The world must see the lustre of that Army restored; and so Pétain sanctioned two successful, if limited battles at Verdun and Malmaison. Respect, confidence and the fighting spirit had come back.

They brought with them the old craving for glory. Pétain was thorough, but, except in his personal bearing, he was not spectacular. The people wanted a leadership that was exuberant, and there was a marked change when, on November 15, Clemenceau became both Prime Minister and Minister of War. He was 76 and a sick man, but the old adversary of the General Staff showed at once that he meant to make the Ministry of War an instrument of victory, and every day he saw Foch as Chief of the General Staff.

He went to the front as often as possible, and the car which took him from the rue Saint-Dominique became a familiar object to the people of Paris. Delightedly soldiers returned his gruff salutation when, in a long black coat and shabby black hat, he walked arm-in-arm with the neat and prim Commander-in-Chief. Pétain soon felt the benefit of a dynamic leadership. 'General Pétain is under my orders,' Clemenceau said in the Assembly. 'I back him entirely.' He backed him, too, in the plan for amalgamating the American regiments within the French Army, and he was furious when Joffre, now a Marshal, emerged from dignified retirement to support Pershing's over-riding objections.

Yet the temperamental differences were obvious to many who saw the Prime Minister and the Commander-in-Chief together. Clemenceau was impatient and, when confronted with an obstacle, his first thought was to scale it. He lacked Pétain's capacity to see a problem in all its bearings. The Commander-in-Chief, never afraid to be called a pessimist, included defeat and failure in his calculations. For reports and dispatches he chose his words so exactly that few could have improved them; but he was not always quick in repartee, and sometimes he was tongue-tied. He feared the politician who might get the better of him in verbal argument. He knew the mind of the fighting soldier, but, unlike Foch, he remained throughout his life wary of the ways of the great world.

In younger years Foch had dared to call on the Prime Minister and to ask bluntly for the directorship of the Staff College, and those early encounters showed him the weaknesses in the old armour. Clemenceau was himself a hot-blooded fighter and ready to forgive impudence or tactlessness in another. When he asked Pétain a question he got a measured or an exhaustive answer; but when he said something to the Chief of Staff, Foch was too eager even to finish his sentence. He relied upon expressive gestures. He hungered for action. He had, moreover, an advantage denied to Pétain, for Clemenceau received the Chief of Staff every day and began to see the war through his eyes.

Foch's judgment was, indeed, finely tempered by the harsh realities of attrition. Yet he still had the exuberance of a thrusting cavalry officer. He saw intuitively the shape of the coming struggle on the Western front. Like a simple man of faith, he had poured out his heart in prayerful gratitude when America entered the war. He was, none the less, certain that Russia would soon make a separate peace with Berlin and with Vienna; and then Ludendorff would hurl many more divisions against the French and the British. France must be strong in man-power and in weapon-power; but in the last terrible offensive she must summon to her aid the whole powers of courage, faith and the will to conquer. If there was antagonism between Foch, the ardent Catholic, and Clemenceau, the impenitent anti-clerical, there was sympathy as well. It lay, perhaps, unrecognized until there was danger.

In frank talks with his personal military adviser, General Mordacq, Clemenceau readily agreed that the French, British and American armies must be welded firmly together. The three national armies, he was certain, should be under a supreme commander, and that chosen leader should be Foch; but he had to wait for the right moment. Early in 1917 Lloyd George backed a proposal that Nivelle should be generalissimo, but the proposal angered Haig and was firmly vetoed by Sir William Robertson, the Chief of the Imperial Staff. The British would hesitate before making a similar proposal. His best ally, Clemenceau thought, would be German cannon; and before dawn on March 21, the cannonade began. Ludendorff was delivering what he believed to be the knock-out blow.

Soon the strain around Roye, at the junction between the British and the French forces, became almost unbearable. Pétain sent three, and then four, divisions to the help of the British, but the pressure against the Fifth Army under General Gough was remorseless The strain, moreover, revealed in sharp outline the differences of aim between Pétain and Haig. Pétain thought, first and foremost, of Paris. Haig worried over the Channel ports, and when he heard that Pétain had considered withdrawing his troops to the south-west in order to cover Paris he wired to London for immediate help and advice. The time had clearly come for some unity of command, and Lord Milner, Lloyd George's right-hand man in the War Cabinet, crossed the Channel with Sir Henry Wilson, now Chief of the Imperial General Staff. Wilson shared with Haig the outlook and the tastes of an Edwardian. He could be intimate with Foch, but not with Pétain; and he argued with Milner that Foch had the right qualities for a supreme commander.

Nor was Foch letting opportunity go by. He went straight to Clemenceau and tried to show that he was the soldier of the hour.

His confidence contrasted strangely with the undisguised anxieties of Pétain, who shocked Clemenceau by telling him that the British might be destroyed in the open field. No Commander-in-Chief, the Prime Minister replied, should say such things, nor even think them. He forgot that Pétain had never used comfortable words.

Four days after Ludendorff began his offensive Poincaré left Paris to preside over the most hurried and the most critical Allied conference of the war. At Compiègne he listened while Pétain made a chilling survey of the struggle; and the guns which were bombarding the town underscored his words. At Doullens, on the following day, Pétain made another realistic statement. This time Milner was more concerned with his manner than with his arguments. It was a desperate hour, and he was in France to decide who should be supreme commander—Pétain or Foch. He watched Pétain closely and noted his air of 'coldness and circumspection'. He saw also that Foch was listening impatiently. Then his mind was made up. So was Haig's.

'If General Foch will give me his advice,' the English soldier said, 'I will gladly follow it'; and before the conference ended Foch was charged with 'the co-ordination of the Allied Armies on the Western Front'. 'I believe', Clemenceau declared, 'we have worked well for victory.' But Foch, when at last he reached his home in Paris, said: 'Pray God, it is not too late.'

Even before the decision was actually reached Pétain let Clemenceau know that he offered no opposition; he would obey all instructions. In later years, when occasionally he was caught off his guard, he might speak scornfully of his treatment by the British. They did not understand him. Nor, perhaps, did he understand them. Deep in his own heart he knew that he was not the man to keep two or three racial teams together. Foch was an imaginative Celt from the far South, and he took liberties beyond the scope of a plain-spoken northerner. Pétain hid his disappointment behind a soldier's dignity, and at once he cancelled his tentative orders for a withdrawal to the south-west.

He did more, for as soon as he reached his headquarters he read

E

reports which told him that the Germans were taking four divisions westwards out of their reserve behind the Champagne line.
He retaliated promptly by ordering nine divisions from his centre
and his right to go to the aid of Fayolle's heavily battered Army
Group. A front nearly four hundred kilometres long—from the
Oise to Alsace—was now held by only sixty divisions; but Pétain
took this calculated risk because he understood aright the minds
both of Ludendorff and of Foch.

He was still the Commander-in-Chief. The new co-ordinator,
with Maxim Weygand as the brains of a minute staff, did not pretend to be the personal director of the French Army, even though
he was the supreme Allied commander. Whether Foch failed or
succeeded—and many desperate hours and days lay ahead—
Pétain would serve France to the end. Meanwhile Clemenceau
made Foch his man. He told the Chamber once that they would
stand or fall together, though later, when the Germans crossed
the Marne, he thought seriously of dismissing Foch.

But the second battle of the Marne was, like the first, decisive.
In the exaltation of coming victory Foch was made a Marshal of
France, and Pétain was given the Military Medal. 'You who love
the soldier and are loved by him', the President of the Republic
told Pétain, 'will wear with a just pride this insignia of courage.'
For Poincaré believed that the cascade of triumphs in the field
demanded eloquence. A few weeks later when Germany's defeat
seemed to be imminent, Poincaré sent his liaison officer to Pétain
with the request that he should make his official communications a
little more vibrant. 'No,' Pétain replied firmly. 'I want to give
only the strict truth, and without any phrases.'

By mid-October final victory was so clearly in sight that Foch
began wrestling with two problems. One was a new offensive to
bring Allied troops to Munich by Christmas Day. The other was
the preparation of armistice terms. On October 28 Pétain joined
Haig and Pershing at Senlis to discuss with Foch the first draft
of the terms. Haig thought that they were too hard for the
Germans to accept, but Pétain wanted them to be more severe.

An armistice, he knew, was a charter defining new rights; it was not an unconditional surrender. It set out the demands of the victors, while leaving a limited freedom to the conquered. Pétain insisted, therefore, that the German army should retire to the Rhine and that the Allies should follow at a day's march behind it. There must be no armistice until the enemy had left France. The terms must be signed on German soil.

Though Pershing backed him, Pétain did not win his way, and on the morning of November 8 six Germans entered a railway dining-car to hear Weygand reading, clause by clause, the terms of the armistice. The setting was strange, and so was the locality. The railway clearing in the forest of Compiègne was far from the Rhine, but only forty miles from the heart of Paris. 'Undefeated on land or sea': such was Kaiser Wilhelm's claim when he wrote his 'Memoirs' in the seclusion of Doorn. Through lack of understanding, the German soldier thought that his own people had stabbed him in the back, but, despite the agony of attrition, the savage and wasteful bloodspilling, he was beaten at last by a method of warfare which Napoleon had clearly discerned. It was blockade: the technique of cold warfare.

Exactly a week after the signing of the armistice Pétain entered Metz at the head of a column of victorious soldiers. He wore no decoration save the Military Cross, and he rode superbly on a white horse. The people cheered with a wild frenzy, and when the General came into the square the deep-sounding bell of the Cathedral boomed over the city. Next day the papers announced that Pétain would be made a Marshal of France. On the 21st Poincaré, a proud Lorrainer, went to Metz, where he handed the Marshal's baton to Pétain before an enormous crowd in the stadium. Five days later the visitor to Metz was Foch, once a student at St Clement's. 'I should not like to die', he had said, 'until I could hang up my sword, as a votive offering, in Metz Cathedral.'

A Marshal of France becomes a legend, and of the three—Joffre, Foch and Pétain—the last was the best-known to the soldiers. He had touched their lives at Verdun and during the mutiny.

They recognized his massive simplicity. He might be stern, but he was also fatherly and understanding. Once he entered a front-line hospital, where he saw a wounded soldier feebly beckoning to him.

'Only eighteen,' the chief medical officer whispered. 'Both lungs pierced. Quite hopeless.'

Pétain walked over to the lad. 'What do you want, my friend? Can I do anything for you?'

'I should like to see my mother.'

'You shall see her. I give you my promise.'

He turned to an ordinance officer and said: 'Take down the address. Send a telegram to the mother. Give orders to all the authorities to let her pass. And send me the account.'

He was 62 and unmarried. By remaining unmarried he could have enlarged the legend of the bachelor-Marshal who treated the soldiers of France as though they were his own sons; he was a stickler for the truth without embellishments. He had not wanted to be Benedict. When he was a captain without influence or family connections, he fell in love and he asked the girl's father for her hand in marriage. The father decided that the prospects before the young officer were unpromising. He refused his consent, and his daughter became Madame Vardon.

Pétain declared that he would marry no other girl. He did not cease to love, and when the war was over, it was Annie Vardon whom he made Madame la Maréchale Pétain.

CHAPTER FOUR

TROUBLED PEACE

ON the 130th anniversary of the storming of the Bastille—July 14, 1919—vast crowds watched the victory parade through the streets of Paris. There were tumultuous cheers both for Pétain as well as for Foch. Untold thousands of them had passed through the mincing-machine of Verdun. From a long collective suffering emerged a hero called the unknown warrior. Yet anonymity was not enough. The people wanted a hero living in the flesh, and that man was the commander though his words were as cold and as precise as his manner

Only five years beforehand Colonel Pétain had ridden on horseback through the streets of St Omer and felt the thrill of pride whenever a schoolboy from St Bertin's gave him a salutation. But for the murders in Sarajevo the war might have come more than a year later. Then, emerging from retirement, the dry-as-dust colonel would have offered to serve at any post available to a pensioned officer. Fame was the reward of diligent study, preparation, shrewdness and independence of judgment, but there was luck as well. The new Marshal owed something to a majesty of bearing. No horseman looked more imposing as he rode towards the Arc de Triomphe and stiffly acknowledged the cheers. Did he find in the applause of the multitude or the approach of humble people a consolation for the veiled disdain of the nimble-witted and the well-born? It is dangerous to acquire a sudden influence or prestige in the early evening of a life hitherto uneventful. To be clothed in legend is to be made unreal.

Foch, the crowds noticed, looked detached and thoughtful. He

had, after all, a problem on his mind. He was not vindictive, and
he had wanted an early peace to follow a quick armistice, 'so that
the wheels of industry should be started in motion throughout the
world'. He argued that three things alone needed to be clearly
settled: Germany's payment of an indemnity, her armed strength
and her frontiers. He wanted to fix her indemnity at a hundred
milliard of marks—twenty times the sum demanded of France
after the 1870 war—and her armed strength at a hundred thousand
men summoned to the colours for one year's service. Most delegates at the peace conference had thought these proposals mild,
but they were astonished by Foch's views on Germany's frontiers,
for he began by asking for the Rhineland. France, he argued, must
have the water-line for her frontier. 'Any other fontier is bad for
us, and may give us illusory security, but not real security.'

He was voicing an old French sentiment. Unless she held the
left bank of the Rhine, Chateaubriand had said a century beforehand, an eight-days' campaign could bring France to her fall.
Whoever held the bridges of the Rhine, Foch insisted, 'is master
of the situation. He can easily repulse invasion and, if attacked,
can carry the war into the enemy's country.' Yet he did not win
his way. 'We don't want another Alsace-Lorraine,' Lloyd George
told him in London, and when Foch talked with Woodrow Wilson, he found him more concerned with the principle of national
self-determination than with frontiers based on military need. He,
therefore, changed his ground and asked for a separate confederation of all the Rhenish provinces. The confederation would be a
new Low Country, and it would be freed from all German control. Not one armed German was ever to set foot on the left bank
of the Rhine.

Clemenceau sympathized with Foch. He knew the strength of
French sentiment about the Rhineland, and he feared Germany's
powers of recovery. Victory must be solid and durable. Yet
Clemenceau had lived in a France perpetually divided against herself, and when the danger of defeat was over the old anti-clerical's
suspicions of the General Staff came once more to the surface. The

Marshals who swaggered into glory owed their batons to the favour of statesmen. The American and the Welshman with whom Clemenceau was now wrangling nearly every day irritated him by their inability to look closely at the physical map of France, but he shared their view that peace-making and the drawing of frontiers were not the concerns of a soldier. He made Foch keep his distance.

But Foch's ambitions were far from Napoleonic. He believed simply that it was his duty always to present the military needs of France, and so he protested when he heard that Clemenceau was ready to give up the demand for a thirty-years' military occupation of the Rhineland for the sake of an Anglo-American guarantee of France's frontier. What, he asked, was the military value of this guarantee? It would take the British a year, and the Americans two years, to send an army to France. The 'solid reality of the guard on the Rhine', he complained, was sacrificed for an alliance 'nebulous in the extreme'. The tension between him and the statesman increased until at last Clemenceau threatened to deprive him of the supreme Allied command and to give it to Pétain.

Even when the peace treaty was ready, there was danger; for the Germans let it be known that they might refuse to sign the document. Refusal would have meant the end of the armistice, and the statesmen decided that Foch must arrange for a march on Berlin. Foch, knowing that the difficulties were excessive, made a disconcerting reply. In his anger Clemenceau sent for Pétain. He got, as he must have expected, a most pessimistic answer. The morrow of victory had swiftly accentuated the dichotomy of statesman and soldier, and when the treaty was formally signed in Versailles, Pétain and Foch were both absent.

The victory parade was a fleeting pageant. Paris is a working city, and on most days of the week Marshal Pétain walked to his office, close to Foch's, in the Boulevard des Invalides. He often passed the railway dining-car in which the German plenipotentiaries had signed the armistice terms. If he had had his way there would have been no signing of an armistice on French soil, and now the dining-car was displayed as a trophy of victory less than a hundred yards away from Napoleon's grave. The French hugged their trophies, but they muffled the glory of their living Marshals, and with the coming of peace Pétain exchanged the high-sounding title of Commander-in-Chief for that of Vice-President of the War Council.

There was no need now to plan a march on Berlin. Soldiers were impatient to return home. From them and from their families came many complaints that the process of demobilization was too slow. Pétain feared that it was too swift. He knew that many factory workers were made restive by the change from war production to the insecurity of free enterprise. Many thousands, influenced by Communist teaching, longed to make common cause with the home-coming soldier. They found him indifferent and unheroic. He was looking backwards, not forward His chief anxiety was to recapture the world as he knew it before 1914 and to return to his old job or to the farmstead. He tried to forget the chilly, evil-smelling battle-line, and he soon lost contact with comrades who were still waiting for their discharge. Everywhere peace was making the levels of life more prosaic.

The long process of demobilization was barely completed when André Maginot, as Minister of War, invited Pétain to become Inspector-General of the Army, while retaining his duties as Vice-President of the War Council; and though he had reached the middle sixties, the Marshal readily accepted. The post gave him his chance to redress evils and to break bottlenecks which vexed him in the war years. Almost his first task, he decided, must be to work out in advance the right relationship between Prime Minister and Commander-in-Chief. It would be necessary to choose beforehand a supreme inter-allied commander and to dovetail the activities of soldiers, sailors and airmen. Co-ordination was the best means of ensuring speed in a time of emergency.

To make ready for speed, however, Pétain had to exercise his long patience and to endure a rapid succession of War Ministers

who came and went before they had grasped their military problems. The Chamber made an exacting sovereign. Deputies
studied the electors and claimed to know the political mind of
France. It was a time of deep frustration, for when the American
Senate refused to ratify the peace treaty the guarantee offered by
Wilson and Lloyd George came to nothing. France, denied both
the Rhineland and the Anglo-American guarantee, faced the old
enemy who would soon be stronger than her victor: all the sacrifices on the Marne and the Somme and before Verdun, it seemed,
had been in vain. There ought to have been increased vigilance.
Instead, there was apathy or defeatist questioning, and Pétain was
asked to plan a reconstruction of the Army in such a way that
compulsory military service could be reduced from two years to
eighteen months.

He protested strongly. With many concise arguments he tried
to show how and where the efficiency of the Army would suffer.
Soldiers were needed to police Indo-China and wide territories in
Africa. They were needed for the Rhineland. Above all, they were
needed for the defence of France, whose vital industries lie close
to her exposed north-eastern frontier. There was also the danger
that one day statesmen might strain the resources of the Army for
some political adventure; and, in fact, Pétain had scarcely begun on
his plan for Army reconstruction when he was suddenly faced with
the exacting demands of Poincaré's policy towards beaten Germany. The office of President of the Republic, which Poincaré
held throughout the war, was too decorative for a man of his
sharp character. He craved the exercise of real power, and two
years after he ceased to be President he became Prime Minister.
His fear and hatred of Germany was as intense as Clemenceau's
and, as he had a legal training, he treated her like a fraudulent
bankrupt. Since she failed to pay impossible reparations, he would
be the lawyer who applied the screws.

First, in mock innocence, he arranged that coloured troops
should be stationed in the Rhineland. Then he decided that Allied
troops must occupy the Ruhr. It was a fateful step, and Bonar

Law, Britain's dying Prime Minister, refused to support it. By his
maladroit policy Poincaré bared to the whole world the cleavage
of aims between the French and the British. Yet none could dissuade him, and early in January, 1923, French troops, fifty thousand
strong, marched into the Ruhr. With them went the Belgians and
a large contingent of Moroccan troops from the Rhineland. No feelings were spared, and at short notice the unhelping British learned
that French troops from Bonn and Wiesbaden were to pass through
Cologne, the headquarters of their own army of occupation.

The inhabitants of the Ruhr numbered nearly four millions,
and if the French imagined that they would be submissive, the
awakening was rude. Pétain, as Inspector-General, made frequent excursions to the occupied Ruhr, and with his own eyes he
saw how the police and all other officials were obeying orders from
Berlin to offer passive resistance. The railways stopped running,
and half a million coalminers were ready to put down their tools.
The French imposed their own authority. They cramped education by seizing schools as barracks. They set up a customs barrier
between the Ruhr and the rest of Germany. They expelled all the
police and officials who had refused to work with them, and in a
vain attempt to set the workers against the industrial leaders they
arrested Krupp von Bohlen and sentenced him to fifteen years'
imprisonment. Yet the German mood did not change, and open
defiance was accompanied by persistent sabotage, a sullen slowing
down of all the wheels of industry, many unexpected and aggra-
vating faults of routine. The Germans were still fighting, and even
in a new method of warfare they showed their skill.

Yet the adventure in the Ruhr did not check the pacifist ten-
dencies within France. Pétain protested once more against limiting conscription to eighteen months; but he knew the mind of the
old soldier who was back in his vineyard and wanted to have no
more dealings with war. He accepted the mood of the country as
a challenge, and with his meticulous thoroughness he completed
the plan of the changes which a new conscription law would involve. The Parliamentary vote was given on April 1, 1923.

No civil disobedience movement lasts for ever, and Gustav Stresemann, when he became Chancellor, called it off, well knowing that the victors were denied their moral triumphs. French deputies, too, grew weary of a lawyer's methods, and they exchanged Poincaré for the Mayor of Lyons, Edouard Herriot. In the end they agreed that the last French soldier should leave the Ruhr by July, 1925. Long before that date was reached, however, Hubert Lyautey, now himself a Marshal, was sending one telegram after another to Painlevé, the Minister of War, telling him that without ample reinforcements he could not prevent Abd-el-Krim, the master of the Riff, from seizing great Moroccan cities like Fez and Taza.

Lyautey knew as much as Pétain or Foch about the vicissitudes of a soldier's fortune. He, too, had feared the days when General André was Minister of War. He was then in France, and he received a telegram which ordered him to report to the Minister of War on the following morning. 'My poor colonel,' said a general, 'can you remember having done anything wrong?' A few days beforehand, Lyautey admitted, he had attended a requiem mass in Alençon Cathedral for Pope Leo XIII. 'We need not look further than that,' the general replied. 'We shall not see you again.'

Instead of punishment, Lyautey got the difficult command of Ain Safru, the westernmost outpost of Algeria. There he looked across the doubtful border of Morocco, the country which he longed to enter. His chance came when, in 1904, an agreement known as the Entente Cordiale allowed Britain a free hand in Egypt and France a free hand in Morocco. The imaginative soldier was ready, and he entered the country as a Christian eager to invest the Moslem with the sword of peace, to be great with the great and humble with the humble. Morocco was his kingdom.

Within him raged constant war between the soldier and the administrator. He believed that a fighter should be bold. He also believed that the way to rule was to woo and to win. The kingdom must rest upon consent; the administrator governs by observing the customs of the people and by respecting their traditions. Whenever he set out for the Sultan's palace he was magnificently mounted and he wore a flowing black burnous with gold fastenings. Yet he often walked alone in the streets of Rabat and talked with a passer-by.

He knew that Pétain, as the peace-time Inspector-General, was struggling to increase the efficiency of the Army, while a new conscription law pruned its man-power. He helped by making his demands for Morocco as few and as simple as possible. The smallness of his garrison was, in fact, a tribute to his skill as an administrator. In 1921 the garrison in Morocco numbered 95,000 men. Two years later, after troops had entered the Ruhr, it numbered 64,000 men.

Lyautey accepted the reduction, for he was certain that his way of working with the Arab and the Berber paid a handsome dividend. People under his Roman rule felt the glow of prosperity, and they were content. But, far beyond Rabat, were districts too remote and too unruly for the Roman peace to touch; and to the north, embracing the Riff mountains and skirting the Mediterranean, lay the Morocco that was Spanish, and not French. Before the war Abd-el-Krim, son of a Kaid and a student at Fez, offered his services to the Spaniards. At first they were gladly accepted, but later the Spanish commander, General Silvestre, came to distrust Abd-el-Krim and sent him to prison.

The young man never forgave the Spaniards who had humiliated him. He was a born leader and, on succeeding his father as the Kaid of a Berber tribe, he preached a war against the Spanish infidel. In 1921 he defeated General Silvestre in battle and by seizing a vast amount of modern arms he soon made himself the master of the Riff. Early in 1925 he began to challenge the French. He meant to capture Fez and Taza and to bring the swelling ranks of his followers to the footholds of the Atlas. His generalship was too good to be ignored, and Lyautey, who had long kept an eye on him, insisted that the rebel must be beaten in the field. No matter how great the threat to Fez or to Taza might become, there must be no withdrawal. The tricolour must not be dishonoured by the sacrifice of a single Moroccan city.

Officers in the threatened zone—they included Colonel Giraud, Captain de Lattre de Tassigny and Captain Juin—shared these views. The Sultan begged Lyautey to believe that his people longed for Abd-el-Krim's defeat. The workers in the cities, it was argued, liked the ordered and way the regularity of their wages, while students delighted in the prospects of a visit to Paris or employment in France. The Resident-General still walked alone and unarmed through the streets. Yet the Roman peace assuaged, and did not destroy, the pride of race. Gusts of hatred swept unaccountably through Lyautey's kingdom. Abd-el-Krim held the sword of Islam, and he would drive the infidel, Spanish or French, back to his own homeland and continent.

Officers like Juin or de Lattre de Tassigny scarcely needed to await orders from Lyautey. He had encouraged them all to ride roughshod over regulations and to act with simple directness. If they wore gloves of velvet, their swords were as sharp as their wits. The time for ease of manner was over. Lyautey's officers would answer in his own language the Kaid who chose to fight. They would defeat a Berber people in the field of battle without provoking their moral resentment. The sword was arbiter.

But the sword is also a figure of speech, and French courage or dash was no protection against the bullets of well-armed tribes-men. They needed more fire-power and more man-power. A Ministry of War which had spread its military tentacles through the Rhineland and into the Ruhr was now confronted with Lyautey's urgent telegrams. The Ministers, not daring to face the deputies with the likely news that a city in Morocco had been lost to Abd-el-Krim, sent Painlevé flying to Rabat. Painlevé returned as swiftly as he had gone, and he begged Pétain to go out and to decide with Lyautey what measures were necessary. Already Pé-tain had withdrawn the Moroccan troops from the Ruhr, and he was hastening the withdrawal of nearly all other troops, so that he might not go to Rabat with empty promises. He soon agreed with

Lyautey that it was not enough merely to compel Abd-el-Krim to retire. The whole Riff must be brought under control.

On his way back from Rabat Pétain passed through Spanish Morocco, where he had a frank talk with General Primo de Rivera. In Paris he amazed the Ministers with the boldness of his scheme; for he planned a full-scale campaign against Abd-el-Krim, which the Spaniards and the French were to wage as allies. The war was to have three phases. The first, lasting to the end of the autumn, would enable the Spaniards and the French to encircle the Riff country. The second, lasting throughout the rainy season, would be marked by intensive propaganda and political action. The third, opening in the spring of 1926, would give the two allies their final victory. Though Pétain was now entering his seventieth year, he had lost none of his precision and capacity for detail. He knew at a glance each military disposition and with what speed ships could be found to take troops and heavy arms to the Moroccan ports. To the astonished Ministers the scheme seemed fool-proof, and they quickly decided that the commander in the field must be Pétain himself. He had no experience of a colonial war, but he agreed to go; and before answering a summons to Paris Lyautey gave him a warm welcome in Rabat.

Pétain was not cosmopolitan, nor was he at ease in a world far from the soil of France. Few commanders understood better the needs of the ordinary French soldier or realized more fully that he is made of flesh and blood and nerve; and yet, perhaps unconsciously, he drew a firm line between the Frenchman and his neighbour. It was one of the reasons why he had sometimes made Haig nervous of his intentions. He went to Lyautey's kingdom for the practical and urgent task of crippling a rebel. He was the thorough-going 'machine-minder' general, not a Bayard, and Lyautey, on his return from Paris, showed disdain as well as coldness. Pétain felt the estrangement keenly and declared it to be undeserved, but he went on with his job, and when he got back to Paris in November he made the terse announcement: 'Morocco is quiet. Abd-el-Krim is no more to be feared. I proceed to policy.'

Included in his policy was a visit of semi-State to Spain. Primo de Rivera met him at the station, and the King, accompanied by the Queen and the Queen Mother, received him in audience. In the evening a gala dinner was given in his honour at the royal palace and, a day or two later, King Alfonso went with him and Primo de Rivera to Toledo to call on the Spanish Primate. Pétain looked a regal figure himself, and the King, forgetting the old restraints of neutrality, praised the Marshal of France as the 'victor of Verdun'.

The third phase of the Moroccan war began early in May 1926. The result was a certainty, and before the month was over Abd-el-Krim surrendered to the commander at Taza. Once more French arms displayed their magnificence, and during the annual parade through the Champs-Elysees the crowds loudly cheered three men—General Primo de Rivera, the Sultan of Morocco and Marshal Pétain. Seven years beforehand Pétain had shared the cheering with Marshal Foch. The prestige and the powers of supreme Allied commander had been denied him. He was not *persona gratissima* with Haig or Henry Wilson or Milner. But the Spaniards had given him their confidence and praise, and the campaign in the Riff showed that he was the successful co-ordinator of two armies. There was an inevitable stirring of vanity. 'Flattery', wrote Kant, 'is the real destroyer of those who are great and powerful.'

Yet the martial ardour of a crowd was roused only for a moment. Far from realizing the plight to which the eighteen months' military service had put the Army, deputies began to clamour for a new limit of one year's service. They knew that a further reduction was a popular issue. Pétain did not resign. He painted the prospect in the darkest colours, but he was not letting the problem defeat him. He worked out various ways of lessening the shock, and he even suggested that only those men who had served in the Army for longer than the legal period should be eligible as State functionaries; but the will of the people was too strong. On March 31, 1928, the deputies voted for one year's service.

The new Conscription law, Pétain was convinced, spelt danger. The only way of overcoming danger was greatly to improve the training of the regular Army and to strengthen the defences, particularly on the frontier from Basle to the Ardennes. Instruction everywhere had to be brought out of the rut, and Pétain feared that the maxims of the last war might become the snares of the next; for the tank and the aeroplane would give a mobility unknown to the defenders of Verdun. At the Staff College, as it happened, General Moyraud imposed a fashionable doctrine. It was necessary, he declared, to study a given zone so minutely that when the enemy was lured into it he was bound to be beaten. This *a priori* method relied on the superiority of defence over offence and on ample fire-power. It turned Pétain's prophetic heresy of other years into a stilted orthodoxy, and a scornful critic was Charles de Gaulle, now about to leave the Staff College.

De Gaulle had deliberately joined the 33rd Infantry Regiment because Pétain was its colonel. He had also fought at Verdun, where he was badly wounded and taken prisoner. Admiration of his former colonel was soon tempered by a more critical attitude. A restless mind struggled against another that was parental, and de Gaulle saw the shadow of discarded teachings in the *a priori* method. He was sure that no enemy would allow himself to be trapped: 'The enemy is no more stupid than we are. He will also try to find the most favourable ground.'

Before de Gaulle actually left the Staff College he took part in manoeuvres as commander of a Blue Army. He deliberately flouted the *a priori* method, and with his own standards of mobility he achieved success. General Moyrand had to concede the victory to the Blue Army, but his efforts to reduce the offender in rank reached the ears of Pétain. The Marshal sent for de Gaulle, listened to his explanations and asked for a report, which the younger man could take a fortnight to prepare. The report pleased him, and he arranged for its writer to go back to the Staff College as a lecturer. He attended de Gaulle's first lecture and later appointed him to his own staff.

Some men are born for the soldier's life. It is their vocation; and Pétain argued that the best men could still be drawn to the Army, if only the conditions of service were made more attractive. The bearing of arms, he thought, should be presented as the most honourable and the most daring of all careers. Yet it was not enough that France should have the finest professional army in Europe. She also needed a solid framework of fortifications. She was vulnerable in nearly all the valleys where her rivers flowed towards Germany or Belgium. Experts had done substantial paper work on the defence system, and Pétain was asked to give his judgment on a report which favoured the creation of three 'fortified regions'—Metz, the Lauter and the Belfort gap. He would withhold his verdict, he said, until he had made a personal tour of all the frontier districts from the Swiss border to the Ardennes. He kept his word. Metz, Bitche, Strasbourg and Belfort were his chief stopping places. Each day he drove to a new district and then walked across country, sometimes discussing with an officer or two a feature of the landscape and relating it to the problem of defence. He went back to Paris satisfied that, in the main, the report was sound.

To keep out the old invader France needed both concentric fortifications of great depth and a line of dispersed battle-forts; and gradually, from the scheme of the three 'fortified regions', there emerged the project of an unbroken line from Belfort to the Ardennes. André Maginot, as Minister of War, gave the wall of steel his blessing, and it came to be known as the Maginot Line. The wall, mostly underground, ran close to the frontier of Luxembourg and stopped short of the Ardennes, where few roads penetrate the thickly wooded country. The creators of the Maginot Line treated Belgium differently from Luxembourg; but, like Pétain himself, they believed that neither France's future war would be exclusively defensive nor that the Belgians would wait until the moment of invasion before summoning the French to their aid. Belgium would be the spring-board for quick-moving offensive action.

F

Early in 1931, when Pétain was approaching his seventy-fifth
year, he gave up the dual posts of Vice-President of the War
Council and Inspector-General of the Army, and his place was
taken by General Weygand. At the same time the Government
fixed sixty-eight as the age at which the potential Commander-in-
Chief should retire. It was a belated admission that war is the
younger man's profession. Yet Weygand, unwilling that the hero
of Verdun should pass into full retirement, asked him to be his
link with the Air Ministry and the Air Force, and the old man—
a balloon officer at the turn of the century—accepted. On the day,
therefore, that he ceased to be Vice-President of the War Council
and Inspector-General of the Army he became Inspector-General
of Aerial Defence. It was a step down the hierarchic ladder, and
many who read their newspapers on a February morning were
astonished by the change. The war was not so distant that they
easily envisaged Foch's adjutant as tomorrow's Commander-in-
Chief. Yet already Foch was dead, and, one by one, the leaders
of the war years were passing away. The hero of Verdun was left
to tell the people that the next war would be fought in the air and
that it would make almost no distinction between combatant and
civilian. Each factory would be a target. The warnings were serious, but they sounded unreal. A prophet was crippled by the
weight of his own legend.

Thus it was as a legendary figure that Pétain went to the
United States in the autumn of 1931 to represent the French
Republic at the celebrations of the 150th anniversary of American
Independence. Two cruisers took the members of his mission
across the Atlantic to Old Point Comfort, where General Per-
shing waited to greet the Marshal of France. Together they passed
through a number of towns until, on the actual anniversary of
Cornwallis's capitulation, they reached Yorktown.

In Washington Pétain talked for a long time with President
Herbert Hoover. The caller was a soldier and the host was a
Quaker brought up to believe that violence is evil. The chief sub-
ject of their talk was the craft of government, and Pétain came

away from the White House convinced that the Americans were fortunate in their political institutions. They elected their own President and made him, as the head of the State, immovable for four years, so that he faced attacks from the Senate and the House of Representatives without being compelled to give up his administration. He was both President and Commander-in-Chief. Unlike the President of the French Republic, he was no mere figurehead, and the American Government, unlike the French, was not submissive to the absolute rule of an Assembly. Pétain, recalling the days when the Third Republic came to birth, wondered why its creators had not followed the American pattern more closely.

Meanwhile another Republic was demanding attention, and its President—the ageing Field Marshal von Hindenburg—was no believer either in non-violence or in democratic institutions. As far back as 1861, when he was a lad of fifteen, he had been made page to Marshal MacMahon, representative of the Emperor of the French, at the coronation of Wilhelm the First as King of Prussia. He venerated the throne, and it may have dismayed him when he heard that Marshal MacMahon had agreed to become President of the new French Republic. Throne and army stood above all statesmen. They stood even above the monarch. and in the war years Hindenburg had forced an unwilling Kaiser to get rid of his Chancellor, Theobald von Bethman Hollweg. By the free decision of the German people, he was the President of their Republic: a monarchist and a soldier vested with powers to dismiss and to choose a Chancellor. The people elected him because defeat in war did not mark the end of Germany. He was the symbol of her continuity and unity. Amid the strains and stresses of a baffled nation he kept a rock-like calm. In January 1933, he sent for Adolf Hitler.

The future had suddenly become ominous. Two Marshals of France—Pétain and Lyautey—talked things over. They were troubled by the sway of pacifist sentiment at home and by the menacing methods of Germany's new master. Their last meeting, in Rabat, had been cold and distant; but now, in the evenings of their lives, they sought reconciliation. After a short silence Lyautey took Pétain by the arm and said: 'Between us there is France.'

CHAPTER FIVE

EVENING

HINDENBURG had met his match. Within a year of Hitler's arrival at the Chancellery he retired to Waldeck, the estate given to him by a grateful nation, and few expected to see him in Berlin again. He almost longed for death, to which, in German fashion, he gave the name of Freund Heinz. 'Has Freund Heinz come into the house yet?' he asked.

'No,' his doctor replied. 'He is not in the house yet. But he is prowling round the garden.'

Every day he read the Bible, looked sadly across his park and prayed that Germany might be delivered from evil. While he lived, and he was eighty-eight, he gave a little hope to thousands who hated Hitler. They imagined that luminous wisdom, not mental enfeeblement, was the crown of patriarchal age.

In Berlin the French had a shrewd Ambassador, André François-Poncet. He, too, hated Hitler, for his Embassy was overwhelmed with reports of imprisonments and beatings. He knew the diplomatic world too well to underestimate the intruder's diabolical cunning and deceit. He refused, therefore, to believe that the Chancellor was a fleeting figure. He had read *Mein Kampf*, and now the wild genius had been given his power to change the face of Europe.

Hitler took Germany out of the League of Nations without explicitly denouncing a Disarmament Conference. He asked that Germany should have a fuller, though limited, armed strength. The French Ambassador knew that he would cheat and that the Germans were secretly arming all the time, but he thought that an agreement with Hitler would provide a means of controlling him. The alternative would be the lack of any machinery of control. The race for armaments would then become furious; and the Ambassador left for Paris to tell the Foreign Minister, Louis Barthou, what was in his mind.

'You have finished by persuading me,' Barthou told him. Then he raised his finger to the ceiling, above which the Prime Minister, Gaston Doumargue, had a private office. 'You must say all this up there. There is the man you must convince.' Before seeing the Prime Minister, François-Poncet called on an old friend who had served on Foch's minute staff as an interpreter. He was André Tardieu, now Minister of State. Tardieu was almost brutal in his frankness. 'You are wasting your time,' he said. 'The convention which you favour will never be concluded, for we shall never be a party to it. Hitler won't last much longer. His fate is sealed. Any convention with him would consolidate his power. Should war break out, not a week would elapse before he would be deposed and replaced by the Crown Prince. You have not summed up the situation properly. I advise you not to insist.'

Military opinion was no less emphatic. 'You will see', the Chief of the General Staff told the Ambassador, 'how long it will take Germany to catch up with the twenty billions we have spent on armaments.' And when at last François-Poncet got his interview with the Prime Minister it brought no encouragement. Doumargue talked; he did not listen. His mind was made up.

He believed himself to be a strong and knowledgeable man, and he had formed his administration in an hour of danger. Nazi propaganda was stirring the embers of racial hatred outside Germany, and early in 1934 Stavisky, a man of unusual charm, was accused of malpractices with the municipal pawn shop at Bayonne. Attempts were at once made to implicate the Government. There were ugly scenes in the Place de l'Opera and outside the Palais Bourbon. Rather than face censure in the Chamber Edouard Daladier, the Prime Minster, resigned, together with the other members of his administration. President Lebrun decided that the hour demanded an administration of full national unity. Only a former head of the State, he thought, could rise above the claims of party. But Poincaré, once the obvious candidate, was now dying. There remained Gaston Doumergue; and while the crowds were still shouting in the streets he chose his team.

He asked General Demain to find out whether Pétain was willing to be a member, and an officer on the Marshal's staff gave the advice that he should be invited to become the Minister of State charged with the mission of co-ordinating the Army, the Marine and the Air Force. Demain could not agree. The ex-President, he said, wanted to form a Government 'without complications and without innovations'. Late in the evening Doumergue sent Pétain a formal offer. He was to have the Ministry of War, but it was on the understanding that any scheme for co-ordinating the three Defence Ministries must go into cold storage. The old soldier, now within three months of his seventy-seventh birthday, wanted to refuse. He feared ceaseless encounters with the Chamber. He was even afraid that the new Ministers might wish to reduce the size of the Army still further so as to meet some future agreement reached at the Disarmament Conference. General Weygand urged him to accept. The year ahead, he said, was critical for the Army. 'The President told me that the country needs me,' Pétain said to the members of the Press. 'I am not stealing away, but I have never concerned myself with politics, and I do not want to do so.'

He moved from his office in the Boulevard des Invalides to the stately apartment, in the rue Saint-Dominique, where General André once meted out punishment to suspected royalists, where Lyautey revived for the fallen Joffre the grand title of Marshal of France, where Painlevé ordered the dismissal of Nivelle, and where Maginot consented to a scheme of gigantic underground fortifications. Each morning the new Minister received the Chief of the General Staff, General Gamelin, and discussed the reports coming to Paris from beyond the Rhine. Little in the routine affairs of the Army was unfamiliar to the Marshal, for he had never

gone into retirement. He was accessible to all comers, and at a
glance he knew who were helpful and who were merely self-seek-
ing. Acquaintances noticed that he had become more mellowed
and paternal, and the coldness of other years seemed to have
dropped like a mask. He was at ease, too, with the journalists, who
called at the rue Saint-Dominique far more frequently than in the
past, and he begged them to mention him by name as seldom as
possible.

If the Council of Ministers held any terrors for the ageing
novice, they were overcome largely by a friendship with Barthou,
whom he first met near Verdun. The statesman was trying to hide
his grief for a son who had been killed in the fighting, and the loss
roused a gruff, unspoken sympathy. When the war was over
Barthou made Pétain a member of a small, intimate and lively
luncheon club called the Paul Hervieu. Only in the Chamber did
he show an occasional discomfort. He feared the trip of a lawyer's
wit, and he suspected that many deputies were vote-collectors
rather than champions of honest views. It was second nature to
him to express views straightforwardly and to point out the dangers which lurked in every situation. His life, however simple, was
hierarchic. He listened, but he also commanded. He showed a
strain of impatience with political discussion and when he paid the
funeral tribute to Lyautey in Nancy, he said, 'France has more
need of work, conscience and renunciation than ideas. Too often
ideas divide where effort unites.'

Yet the Chamber was never unfriendly to him, and he was
acclaimed when, in mid-June, he mounted the tribune to ask for a
special credit of 1,275 million francs for military arms. A fortnight
later he had still greater success in the Senate, where only twelve
members voted against the credit. With this encouragement he
began to prepare the way for an extra credit of eight hundred million francs for motorization, anti-aircraft guns, tanks and gas-
masks. It was easier, in fact, to made demands on the Frenchman's
pocket than on his freedom, and General Weygand found that he
was pleading in vain for an immediate change in the law on mili-

tary conscription. Pétain agreed with him that one year's service no
longer allowed France a margin of safety, but he was biding his time.
The old machine-minder general did not under-value the large
credit for military arms; it would turn the thoughts of the industrial worker to the needs of his own country and give France her
start in the race for armaments. Cabinet business, moreover,
could be crowded, and Doumergue was sometimes peremptory
with colleagues.

For while Weygand and Pétain kept their eyes on a secretly
arming Germany, soldiers were no wiser than statesmen in their
judgments of Hitler. He was the contemptible accident soon to be
removed by sober German leaders. What soldier need fear a
demagogue who never rose above the rank of corporal in the Great
War? What statesman of France other than a diligent Ambassador
had troubled to read *Mein Kampf*? It was, indeed, a fantasy that
the corporal of any war should carry the sword, sceptre, orb and
crown of Charlemagne in his knapsack.

Yet 1934 was Europe's crucial year. June 30 was Hitler's night
of St Bartholomew. July 25 marked the murder of Austria's Chancellor, Engelbert Dollfuss. On August 2 the German wireless
announced that Hindenburg was dead and that Hitler was invested
with all the functions of the President. Next day Hitler assumed the
titles of Fuehrer and Chancellor of the Reich. All hope of an
appeal from the Chancellor to the President had vanished. Hitler
was Germany's absolute master. The time had come swiftly when
France must rally her friends and consult with them how to meet
a common danger. On October 9 Barthou stood at the quay-
side in Marseilles waiting to greet King Alexander of Yugoslavia
and to conduct him on his State visit to Paris. As the carriage drew
along the Cannebière on the way to the station two Croats shot
dead the King and Louis Barthou.

The double murder was committed just when the newsreelmen
waiting in the famous street had their cameras trained on the King's
carriage, and within a few days cinema patrons in London and
many other cities had a front-seat view of an assassination. They

saw the King falling stiffly backwards and watched the confusion of an angry crowd. The film was not shown in German cinemas. It would not have done for a discontented anti-Nazi to realize with what ease a monarch and a statesman had been put to death; but Goering was fascinated by the film, and he tried to show it to the French Ambassador. It portrayed the incompetence of the police protection which France was offering to her royal visitor.

Already France was caught in the vortex of violence. It was not enough for Doumergue to accept the resignation of Albert Sarraut, the unhappy Minister of the Interior. The country must be handsomely represented at the King's funeral in Belgrade. President Lebrun at once agreed to go, but it was necessary that the most distinguished Frenchmen of the day should accompany him. Pétain was the last of the great commanders in the war which won a flaunted freedom for the people of Yugoslavia; and he went with the President of the Republic in a spirit of stern duty. He knew that for both of them the reception in Belgrade would be formal and chilly. He would brave the ordeal with majestic calm.

At first the Germans selected a diplomatist to represent them at the King's funeral. Then Hitler decided that Goering must go. He arrived with full pomp in Belgrade, and on the bier he laid a wreath inscribed: 'To the heroic adversary of yore—the German Army in heartfelt grief.' He sought out Pétain, and in public he took care to appear at his side as often as possible.

The obsequies were scarcely over when Doumergue's administration of 'national unity' fell. Pierre Flandin, the new Prime Minister, begged Pétain to stay at the rue Saint-Dominique, but the Marshal was not to be persuaded. Age was against him. It was one thing to become a Minister when the Stavisky scandal seemed to be bringing France to the verge of civil war; and it was another to join a new Ministry which meant to give the spirit of party a franker play. Pétain, moreover, felt keenly the death of Barthou, and it had been no comfort to him that Doumergue chose Pierre Laval to take Barthou's place at the Quai d'Orsay.

Laval was the cartoonist's delight. His hair and moustache were ill-kept, and though his clothes were untidy, the whiteness of his cravat accentuated a swarthy complexion. Walrus-like lips often parted into a roguish smile, and whenever he rose to speak, the spell of personality made hearers forget his lack of principle or culture. In younger years he belonged to the extreme Left in politics, and early in the war, which he opposed, he was in danger of imprisonment for his pacifism. A few brief years in the political wilderness enabled him to shed his past as a Social Democrat, and he came back to public life richer and more sagacious. He had risen from poverty to affluence through ways that were adroit or shabby, but few who met him remained untouched by his charm. He treated no man as saint or villian, for all made of human clay had their weaknesses and foibles; and many left his company not realizing that they had fallen from a pedestal. He treated fellow-deputies not as delegates of the people, but as marionettes. He pulled the strings.

Boldness of imagination caused him to see further than his colleagues. Where Barthou had worried about the strength of Poland or the Little Entente formed by Czechoslovakia, Rumania and Yugoslavia, Laval spoke of Russia, Germany and Italy. These were the powers in Europe which counted. Russia might help to keep Germany in check. So might Italy. It was thus absurd to treat the Fascists and their Duce with contempt. The Corporative State, so far as Laval troubled to study it, was not unattractive; it freed the man who liked power or intrigue from the fetters of a constituency. Laval knew how to manage party men. He talked them round. He smiled disarmingly at the critical moment. He became the dominant personality in a crowded room, and his uncouth gestures were forgotten.

Many, indeed, reacted sharply against him, and one among them was Pétain. So far from realizing that Laval treated the Chamber as a farce, the Marshal regarded him as the typical politician, the schemer and party boss. He disliked his lack of attention to details and his want of moral firmness; and he chose to forget how Laval had encouraged him when he stepped down the hierarchic ladder to become the Inspector-General of Aerial Defence. The man of gypsy origin was intuitive and undisciplined; and it was like a bad omen when he succeeded Barthou in the very week that Poincaré died. Pétain shared Weygand's view that the quality of political leadership in France had begun steeply to decline.

He had, however, a stronger reason for his refusal to stay at the rue Saint-Dominique. The war of tomorrow, he was convinced, must be waged by an entirely new generation. The men who had seized power in Germany were mostly young, and Hitler was still in his middle forties. Youth must be pitted against youth, and it was no accident that de Gaulle had joined Pétain's staff. Mobility, pace, quick decision, untiring energy: these qualities sprang from youth.

While Pétain was still at the Ministry of War, de Gaulle published a book called *Vers l'Armée de Metier*, in which he argued the necessity of getting away from the dominant ideas of defensive warfare. All the great War Ministers from Vaubon to Maginot, he frankly admitted, tried to stop the breaches in France's frontiers by fortifications, and though these fortifications were still important, they left the northern frontier unprotected. 'How', de Gaulle asked, 'can you estimate the disastrous effect that modern mechanical weapons might produce on the defenders—dive-bombers, heavy tanks, poison gas?' Modern weapons might impose sweeping change, but de Gaulle knew that the Army was unsympathetic to change: 'The open-mindedness of individuals does not preclude conservation in the body as a whole. The Army lives on stability, conformity and tradition. Instinctively it fears anything that tends to modify its structure.' Yet it must fight the next war with tanks and aeroplanes, and de Gaulle drew his picture of a tank attack.

The tanks, drawn up in battle formation, are arranged in three lines. First are the light tanks to make the first contact with the enemy. Then comes the real battle line of medium and heavy tanks. Behind them is the reserved line. 'Suddenly the monsters are unleashed. The light tanks, springing away from the base, rush forward to make contact with the enemy. Their business is to determine the position and the quality of the first line of resistance, to explore the most favourable approaches, to camouflage by smoke-screen the difficult passages: in short, to reconnoitre and act as cover for the main body. When they have fulfilled their objective the small tanks will disengage and make for the flanks for observation purposes or go to the rear to lay down reconnaissance lines. At each lull in the battle they will take up again their duty as scouts in the vanguard.

'But now the main line in its turn feels its way into the struggle. The large groups of which it is composed deploy over the terrain not in straight lines but in independent sections, manoeuvring according to the situation of the moment. The axis of their advance in most cases will be oblique to the enemy front so as to meet any resisting force at a slant and be free to change their direction many times according to the progress of the battle. These highly mobile units machine-gun the terrain, saving their large guns for pre-determined objectives, which they try to destroy by taking them from the rear. Each movement is designed to flank enemy firing units, to attack them from behind, the artillery covering the action by fire distributed all around the zone of attack and hiding by smoke-screen the tanks that remain stationary.'

Meanwhile the forward movement is not cramped too much by mopping-up operations. The tanks in the van are used 'just long enough to effect a break-through and push on to the ultimate objective as quickly as possible. Their support will finish what they have started.' If the enemy resists stubbornly the attackers will appear as 'groups of tanks fighting in great depth while the first wave continues towards its objective'. In its attack the tank has an absolutely reliable partner in the aeroplane, which can strike directly at any target and co-ordinate with the tank in every 'break-through and follow-up'.

Some of de Gaulle's brother-officers, as they read the book, declared that it faithfully reflected Pétain's views. That was true. The style was occasionally more eloquent or more flamboyant than old 'dry-as-dust' would have liked, but the close-knot skeleton of its arguments was almost Pétainist. Mechanization was capable of unending development, and the Marshal readily agreed that the conditions which had forced him to believe in defensive warfare before 1914 were now over. The book which de Gaulle wrote and Pétain sponsored had few readers when it first appeared in 1934. But one of them was Rommel.

The war of the trenches was fading into history, and now its last surviving Marshal must relax his hold upon the affairs of the State. He believed, early in 1914, that he was about to retire. This time his retirement would be genuine. He agreed to remain a member of the High Committee on National Defence, and he wrote an article for the *Revue des Deux Mondes* on the urgency of lengthening the period of military service; but he let it be known that there was still a little life left for him to enjoy. He wanted to taste more fully some of the privileges which his own prestige had brought him. For one thing, he could not give up his visits to Verdun. The city was his fief. He liked to walk reverently through the military cemeteries, and he said that he wanted to be buried with the men who had died at Douaumont. The citizens asked him whether they might erect a statue in his honour. 'No,' he replied sharply. 'Not in my lifetime.'

Since 1919 he had been a member of the Academy of Moral and Political Sciences—the Institute founded by Napoleon for the frank exchange of knowledge—and Pétain liked to hear men speaking on their own subject without the restraint of a report to the newspapers. Once he spoke at the Institute with such clarity on the causes of the mutiny in the Army that several members begged him to publish his paper in the *Revue des Deux Mondes*; and regretfully they remembered that publication was against the rules. The Institute, however, chose him to be one of the three curators of the Chantilly estate, and he was given an apartment in the handsome castle. 'I'm the *concierge* of Chantilly,' he told his friends. He liked the gardens, and he spent many hours talking with the foresters. Once, greatly daring, he installed a telephone in his apartment, and he wondered whether he might fit it with electricity as well.

When Foch died, many assumed that Pétain would be the next Immortal of the French Academy. He wanted to avoid becoming a candidate. He had a right, he argued, to be a member of the Academy of Moral and Political Sciences because war was a science, and he had waged it as a scientist. He did not pretend to be a literary man. Though he weighed each word in his report and was quick to denounce a slovenly statement, he refused to see himself as a guardian of the French language. Yet Foch had followed Joffre at the Academy, and it seemed inevitable that Pétain should now follow Foch. 'The Academy asks you,' Poincaré said, 'and she is an old lady. You cannot offend her with a refusal.'

Like Joffre and Foch, Pétain secured a unanimous election, but eighteen months went by before he presented himself beneath the cupola; and there he heard Paul Valéry call him 'the spirit of the resistance'. In his long tribute to Foch, he admitted that there were divergencies of military doctrine between them, but he praised the 'exceptional appetite for action' which helped Foch to polarize conflicting wills and to give the spirit of unity to a coalition. Paris newspapers published the new Immortal's address in full, but Pétain did not want to read it through again. The tribute, he said, lacked elegance. He belonged more to Napoleon than to Richelieu.

Few men had ever looked more imposing on the parade ground, and Pétain was one of the most photographed men in France. Yet he took long walks through Paris without drawing attention to himself. He liked to go to a cinema or to sit in a café and to watch the people as they went by, absorbed by their daydreams or their anxieties. More than ever, in his old age, he felt the need of the common touch. Only when his life was gliding into the eighties did he lose his delight in Paris; and then he wanted to spend his last days wholly in Villeneuve-sur-Loubet. To abandon all interest in the affairs of France was impossible; for he, too, had the 'appetite for action'. But since fighting was the task for another generation, he pictured the scorn of rising young officers for 'papa Pétain'.

Some of his calculations had already proved to be wrong, and he took the gloomiest view when King Leopold brought Belgium back to her traditional pre-1914 neutrality. Belgium played her part in the occupation of the Ruhr, and he had assumed that she linked her military fortunes with those of France. She was the spring-board which France needed to confound the German attack. Now there was a danger that she would await invasion before summoning help from France, and, impelled by chivalry, the French would move from defensive strength to weakness. The flower of their Army might then be trapped by a German drive to the Channel ports.

The invasion of Ethiopia, the arrival of German troops in the Rhineland, the Anschluss with Austria, the rape of Bohemia: each act deepened the darkness over Europe. The French knew not how to answer the charge that they were Maginot-minded and had lost their old temper of ascendency. General Weygand had seen the forging of firm links between Allied armies when he was Foch's right-hand man; and now that he, in turn, reached retirement he deplored the way in which former partners were estranged. The French and the British alike, he found, were living on legends. The British thought that the French Army was the finest in the world; the French pinned their faith on the Royal Air Force. There was a want of frankness. The one partner made the short-comings of the other an excuse for inaction.

However Maginot-minded the French had become, they knew that the Maginot Line was no barrier to a political philosophy. Totalitarian regimes challenged the sway of Parliamentary democracy and underscored its defects. The kinship of Europe, moreover, was a factor which the French acknowledged. Most of them shared Pétain's pride in the soil of France; but the people of Alsace spoke German, and the casual visitor to Marseilles often fancied that he was in a city as much Italian as French. The Corporative State was an idea capable of export to France.

Thus, early in 1937, Gustav Hervé published a pamphlet which he called *We Want Pétain*. Hungary, Poland, Italy and Germany, he argued, had made war on the Communism which was now threatening the whole of Europe. France needed to follow the example of these countries and to make her Republic authoritarian. If Pétain read the pamphlet, he thought little of it. But Hervé, the author, had been the school friend of Laval; and to Laval the idea of an authoritarian Republic with Pétain as its President was not unattractive. The Marshal would make an admirable marionette, and Laval began to pull the strings. In retirement Pétain scarcely troubled to find out who was playing with his legend. In his heart, perhaps, he knew how often he had allowed ambition to masquerade as duty, but now its fire was burning out. He believed that he had finished with Paris. He merely wanted, he told a correspondent, 'to receive sympathetic friends'.

In their company he spoke his own aged mind. He felt keenly the issues involved in the Spanish Civil War. The exiled King and General Primo de Rivera had been his friends, and his campaign in Morocco ended with the surrender of a rebel against the authority alike of Spain and of France. He knew the quality of the Spanish troops, and though he was the least cosmopolitan of soldiers, he did not deny the Spanish affinity with France. Nor, perhaps, did he deny that the Republicans were vested with constititutional authoity. He saw the conflict, however, as a first round in the war between Communists and the upholders of order. Twenty years beforehand, in his masterly report to Painlevé, he had shown how great a part revolutionary ideas played in the mutiny. Once 'the ferments of revolutionary ideas' spread from distant Moscow: now they were spreading from Madrid. The fears of two decades ago were magnified. In old age the mind becomes less agile or flexible, but it cannot greatly change its physiognomy.

What Pétain thought about the Spanish Civil War was not remarkable. He was a private citizen exercising his right of private judgment. All over France, in fact, men and women were taking

G

sides. The Pyrenees were neither high nor deep enough to contain the tension and excitement. The troubled statesmen of France might face darkly the menace of war on three fronts: on the Rhine with Germany, below the Alps with Italy, and in the footholds of the Pyrenees with militaristic Spaniards. But younger men were not bothering about discretion. The issues of the civil war were much too intimate for them to remain spiritually neutral, and several hundreds crossed the frontier to join the International Brigade.

Many were taken prisoner. They had backed the loser, and there came a day when Edouard Daladier, as Prime Minister, could no longer withhold recognition of the victor who had Hitler and Mussolini for his patrons. An Ambassador must be found for the Spanish Government in Burgos. He must have the right prestige and be the man whom General Franco, the conquering Caudillo, would be glad to welcome. The one man who had the necessary attributes was Pétain. He was the friend of Primo de Rivera, founder of the Falange; he was the vanquisher of Abd-el-Krim, the hero of Verdun, the last surviving Marshal of France. He alone would have the authority to demand, as from one soldier to another, the return of the French prisoners. Daladier made his choice, and General Franco barely concealed his joy.

That joy was reflected by the right-wing newspapers of Paris. The parties of the left, none the less, detested the recognition which their Government had given to General Franco, a rebel against Parliamentary democracy. They wished him still to be treated with scorn. Instead, the hero of Verdun was to go to Spain as Ambassador. 'The most noble, the most humane of our military leaders', wrote Leon Blum in *Populaire*, 'is not in his place as representative to Franco.' Yet most of Blum's readers were troubled about the fate of the French prisoners. No other compatriot was likely to be more persuasive with General Franco. The Marshal would secure the prisoners' return.

Pétain was eighty-two. He scarcely knew the Prime Minister who was dragging him back to public life, and he did not like him.

Yet it was a new call to duty, and the vanity which may have mingled with the response was fanned by the head of the French Government. The Marshal reached Hendaye on March 16, 1939. It was the day after the German troops entered Prague.

The events of that fateful Ides of March could scarcely be misread. A new war in Europe was fast becoming a certainty, and General Franco, untried in victory, might lean dangerously on his German patron. The Ambassador would not flinch in his duty, and, splendidly erect, he walked to the frontier. Great times demand great leaders, and almost as soon as Pétain arrived in San Sebastian he heard that people in Paris were canvassing his name as President of the Republic when Albert Lebrun's seven years of office came to an end. He gave the report little thought, and on March 20 he wrote to General Brocard, telling him: 'I am not a candidate for the Presidency of the Republic.'

He had a definite task before him and, a few days later, the Duke of Saragossa drove the engine of a special train which took him from San Sebastian to Burgos, where he presented his credentials to the Caudillo. Fame preceded him, and when at last the Diplomatic Corps left Burgos for Madrid, the citizens sought many opportunities of greeting the Marshal. They saw him on his morning walk in the Retiro park, where he exchanged a few phrases with a peasant or patted a child on the head. With humble people he was always at ease. Yet he knew when to assume the glacial look of the great commander. He attended the service which marked the reinterment of Primo de Rivera's body in the Escurial; and, as soon as he entered the basilica, the members of the Diplomatic Corps, led by the German Ambassador, all rose to their feet.

Within six months France was again at war with Germany, and Daladier called the Ambassador back to Paris to offer him a portfolio. Pétain refused. He did not make the weight of years his excuse. A soldier is always ready to answer the call to duty. General Weygand, though seventy-two, had offered his services and gone cheerfully to the little important command in Syria. When things are going wrong, Weygand's friends told him, 'they are

bound to send for you. But only when it is too late.' Pétain, however, still could not bring himself to like the Prime Minister, and
his own task in Madrid had only just begun. The war-wearied city
was a vantage-point.

No other Ambassador within its walls read so clearly the lessons
of the assault on Poland. It was lightning war, and the first terrible
accounts were like pages torn from de Gaulle's prophetic book.
With beautiful precision the German tanks leaped forward, and
the dive-bombers were an unfailing escort. No amount of personal
courage or sacrifice could stay their course. The machine was the
master of the fighting man, and nothing done or attempted on the
Western front checked by a single hour the sweep of armour into
the heart of Poland. Within a month military resistance was over,
and Hitler was free to turn his forces to the West. The legend
spread that the German Army was invincible, and Pétain watched
the star of France waning in the diplomatic firmament of Madrid.

Yet Hitler's victory brought dark fear to the Spaniards. The
Fuehrer had leagued with Stalin to destroy a Catholic country:
'crucified', cried an eloquent Polish preacher, 'between two
thieves'. Into Madrid poured reports of Gestapo brutalities.
Hitler's men were showing no mercy to the defeated Poles. They
were Slavs of a second-class citizenry, and in the eyes of the Nazis
they deserved to be treated like galley-slaves. Pétain was all the
more anxious because he recognized that the Polish campaign was
a revolution in the art of war. First came the speed of the tank-
aeroplane combination, to defy the orthodox patterns of linear
defence, and it was followed by the inevitable submission of a
people whose fighting men are beaten in the field. Whether ruled
by Nazi gauleiters or by Soviet commissars, Poland was trodden
underfoot.

Was France to escape a similar fate? Her military machine was
slow-moving. All through his adult life Pétain had experienced
the clustering strength of tradition and the time-lags of discipline.
The Maginot Line was itself a monument of linear defence; it faced
only one way and ended near the Ardennes. Belgium was the

invader's gateway and now, hugging a desperate neutrality, she refused to have any staff talks with the French. If the Germans were to pierce their defences or if discipline were to snap, would the French escape the treatment given to the defeated Poles? It was Pétain's habit, and often his strength, to anticipate the worst misfortunes; and in his mind's eye he saw catastrophe. In March, 1940, he wrote to M. de Monzie and told him, half in irony, that 'they might need me'.

CHAPTER SIX

DEFEAT

WITHIN two months France had need of Marshal Pétain. Paul Reynaud, a friend of de Gaulle, had succeeded Daladier as President of the Council. His fighting spirit contrasted oddly with a lack of physical stature, and one of his first acts was to exchange with Britain a solemn pledge never to make a separate peace with Germany. He knew that there were deep-seated prejudices to be overcome in the High Command, and he believed that he was ready to make some ruthless changes. He summoned General Weygand from Beyrouth for a consultation, and he began to talk freely to him about the shortcomings of the Supreme Allied Commander, General Gamelin.

General Weygand was not responsive, and he showed clearly that he did not want to be General Gamelin's critic. Loyalty was his strongest trait, and he had given Foch an almost selfless devotion. He was the born staff officer, even though he lacked the staff officer's training. It did not follow that he possessed the swift divination of his mercurial old chief, but he had lived near to greatness. With greatness the new Prime Minister wished to be surrounded. He had not misread the lessons of the campaign in Norway; the tanks and aeroplanes which quickly brought another country to subjection would soon menace France. At the end of April he summoned the Ambassador from Madrid. Marshal Pétain reached Paris on May 1 and agreed to become a Minister of State. 'Marshal Pétain is at my side,' Reynaud announced on the radio. 'He will remain there until the day of victory.'

The Marshal's duties were not clearly defined, and Paul Reynaud took for himself the portfolio of Minister of War; but Pétain saw Gamelin and studied the inter-Allied plan for an advance into Belgium on the day of her invasion. He made no protest, for he was careful not to intrude upon the sphere of the Supreme Allied Command. He was a Minister, not a commander, and he acknowledged that he was out of touch with military realities. On May 9 he was back in Madrid to make his farewells, and that night German troops crossed the frontier of Holland, Belgium and Luxembourg.

The Allies did just what the Germans wanted them to do; they leaped forward into Belgium. The tanks of von Rundstedt's Army Corps crossed the Meuse and began to cut them off. Within five days the Dutch resistance was broken. Within seven nothing stood between Paris and some German tanks which had reached Laon; but the Germans were putting the Channel ports before Paris. Each hour told its tale of agonizing surprise, and on May 17 Paul Reynaud once more summoned Pétain from Madrid and Weygand from Beyrouth. Pétain came back to Paris openly expressing his scorn of the rush to Belgium's aid. Since the Belgians had clung to their neutrality and refused staff talks with their neighbours, the French should have stood everywhere on the defensive. 'We are the victims of the neutrals,' the Marshal declared.

Reynaud made him a Vice-President of the Council as well as Minister of State, and the news that he was in Paris again comforted the people. At the eleventh hour, they believed, another Joffre might arise to save them on the Marne. Newspapers told them less than half the truth, for journalists were as bewildered as their readers by the swiftness of the enemy's advance. Among civilians only a few understood the speed and agility of the new warfare, and even for them it was hard to acknowledge that five thousand German tanks and two thousand German aeroplanes were disrupting entire armies. Yet, after the break-through at Sedan, one hundred thousand men, moving rapidly in tank or aeroplane, were to have five million soldiers at their mercy.

Within two days of his summons Weygand reached Paris, where he saw Reynaud and Pétain together. He looked vigorous and sprightly and he was impatient to get to General Gamelin's headquarters to size up the state of affairs for himself. The Supreme Allied Commander said almost nothing. He had the gaze of a man who knows that he is beaten and expects to be dismissed; and it was General Georges, commander of the critical north-east sector, who gave the newcomer a disturbing account of the battle. Weygand hurried back to Paris, and when the Prime Minister and the Marshal, once more together, told him that he must at once assume command, he accepted without a murmur. He was well over seventy, and he had lived in retirement for five years before going out to Syria. Now he was told to retrieve a situation entirely new to him. The task, he said, was not impossible, and he radiated confidence. He was like Foch come back to life.

Everything depended on closing the gap which the Germans had torn in the Allied lines. The divisions isolated in the north must get out of their trap by launching a quick offensive southwards, and less than forty-eight hours after his arrival from Syria Weygand went by aeroplane and road to meet the King of the Belgians and Lord Gort, the British commander, in Ypres. He found the most appalling confusion. Refugees flooded the roads, for in the wake of the advancing German Army Groups went men specially trained to create havoc and despair. King Leopold arrived an hour late, and Lord Gort did not even reach Ypres before Weygand was compelled to leave. By that time conditions were so changed that the general's aeroplane could be left no longer in Calais. Weygand made his way to Dunkirk, and a naval ship, leaving harbour during a heavy air-raid, brought him to Cherbourg. A train got him to Paris in time for the daily conference with Reynaud and Pétain. He was too old, and he had been summoned too late. The offensive which he quickly planned should have been launched while he was still in distant Beyrouth.

For the Germans allowed their foe no respite. The gap was not closed. On the contrary, it grew wider. The British began to withdraw. German tanks reeled round Lille and cut off eight French divisions. The offensive had to be given up. Yet Weygand did not immediately despair. He planned a bridgehead which stretched coastwise from Ostend to Calais and in depth from Courtrai to St Omer. Eight British divisions and one armoured unit, fourteen French divisions and the Belgian Army were to man the bridgehead. Its ports provided supply routes to Britain, and one day the bridgehead would become a springboard for an offensive. But the new Supreme Commander soon discovered that he was making a bridgehead on quicksand. On May 26 German tanks took Boulogne and raced towards Calais. Next day the Belgian Army laid down its arms. The bridgehead had to go the way of the offensive. Soon the evacuations from Dunkirk were in full swing.

On the bomb-swept beaches the soldiers of broken armies pondered on the cruelty of their fate. Man for man, they were as brave as their fathers who fought at Ypres, Vimy or Verdun; but in the unequal struggle with the armoured machine personal bravery counted almost for nothing. Hundreds of ships and boats, large or small, moved through the narrow sea. But why were so few of the aircraft storming in the heavens French or British?

Meanwhile Weygand was organizing a new defence line along the Aisne and the Somme, where, he was certain, the German armoured divisions would soon hurl themselves. In a letter, written on May 29, he gave the Prime Minister the gloomiest picture of his prospects. He saw a desperate threat to Paris. He saw even the collapse of France's military defence; and though he acknowledged that their country stood in danger of immediate invasion, he declared that the British should at once provide two to three divisions as well as tanks, anti-tank and anti-aircraft batteries and 'the co-operation of the air force based in England'. Two days later the Prime Minister answered the letter. The Supreme Allied Commander was to prepare a national redoubt in Brittany. Promptly the harassed general began to make arrangements, and he agreed with Admiral Darlan that the redoubt should include Cherbourg and the Cotentin as well as Brest.

The Breton redoubt was de Gaulle's idea. It did not impress Weygand and he said so. Yet a strong idea was needed to upset the enemy's calculations and to rob him of his initiative. The time had come to draw upon the divisions now almost pointlessly defending the Maginot Line and to put many French tanks and aeroplanes into a daring battle array. France needed commanders with minds attuned to the new warfare and who had not passed the age when Julius Caesar or Napoleon or Wellington revealed the full splendour of military genius. The greatness with which the Prime Minister of France surrounded himself was the greatness of legend. The panzer divisions were not fighting the war of 1914.

On the night of June 3 the Germans reached the harbour of Dunkirk, and the beaches came directly under their fire. The battle of Flanders was almost at an end and the battle of France was about to begin. Nine British divisions were lost. So were thirty French divisions, the entire Belgian Army and vast supplies. Dunkirk was a military disaster, and now the Germans faced the French with a superiority of three to one in manpower and five to one in armoured units. Under the shadow of the new and decisive battle General Weygand bade the troops forget old notions of lines of defence. They were to defend in depth. They were to resist, and whenever the enemy's armour swept past them, they were to form hedgehogs of resistance; but the patterns of past training made too difficult a sudden change in their methods of linear defence. Maginot-mindedness had become ingrained.

The commander had nothing like enough arms or equipment or reserves. He was in desperate need of time in which to consolidate his new defences. Lightning war, however, deliberately denies time to the adversary. Between the battle of Flanders and the battle of France there was a breathing space of less than twenty-four hours; for on June 5 the Germans attacked on the line of the Aisne and the Somme.

At a tense meeting of the War Committee, held only a few hours after the attack had begun, General Weygand complained

that the help coming from Britain was 'derisory', and in an effort
to dispel the gloom General Spears translated a passage from the
speech which Winston Churchil had just made in the House of
Commons. 'We shall go on to the end. We shall fight in France.
We shall fight on the seas and the oceans . . . We shall fight on the
beaches. We shall fight on the landing grounds. We shall fight in
the fields and in the streets. We shall fight in the hills. We shall
never surrender.' For a moment the sense of the meeting was completely changed. 'Your Prime Minister,' Reynaud said to General
Spears, 'was speaking for France as well as for England.'

So he was; but the men and women who cheered him uproari-
ously in the House of Commons were nearly all of them the men
and women who cheered Neville Chamberlain when he announced
Hitler's invitation to Munich. They were the same people, though
their mood had since hardened into resolution. The guns, once
pointed at distant Bohemia, were now thrust deep into France,
and soon they might menace London. Invasion would come when
the battle of France was over. Englishmen and Frenchmen alike
saw a cruel ending to the battle; the English saw it intuitively, and
the French with a bold exercise of their intelligence. France had to
survive; and without air-cover her soldiers could not grapple with
the aeroplane-tank combination. General Weygand begged
General Spears to take back this message to Winston Churchill:
'The battle is lost if it is not prolonged, and it is unlikely that we
can prolong it without fighter aircraft.'

Though Marshal Pétain attended each meeting of the War
Committee, he was usually a silent figure. He did not hear all that
was said, nor did he voice a frequent disapproval. He liked to go
back to his old office in the Boulevard des Invalides, where he
studied a large map and pondered on the mechanics of lightning
war: sixty French divisions fighting against ten panzer divisions
and 120 infantry divisions. The British now had only one division
still fighting in France, and the Marshal scorned the quantity of
their air support. A cancer was rotting in the heart of France, and,
as in the days of the mutiny, Pétain had harsh thoughts about

the politician who fights with words and campaigns with intrigue.

In a dark hour General Spears called at the Boulevard des Invalides to find the Marshal angered by de Gaulle's new appointment as Under-Secretary for War. Pétain complained that de Gaulle was vain, omniscient and ungrateful. 'I know all about him. He was once on my staff and wrote a book, or at least I told him how to do so. I gave him the outline and corrected it, in fact annotated it in my own hand. When he published it he did not even acknowledge my contribution.'

General Spears had called to ask the Marshal to dissuade General Weygand from making so many sharp comments on the British; but the old man, making full use of his deafness, heard only what he wanted to hear. He read aloud a speech on Joan of Arc and made General Spears read another on the peasants of France. Not far away was the smoke and the tumult of a battle likely to spell the doom of France, and the Englishman made one more effort to carry out his self-appointed mission. His countrymen were in deadly earnest, he declared, when they said that they would fight to the bitter end. 'It is possible that one day and for a while, France may be driven to fight back from Africa, as we may be to fight back from Canada and the remainder of the Empire.'

Pétain, making no reply, led his visitor to a small room in which stood a bronzed group. The Marshal on horseback was bending towards two soldiers of the first World War who gazed at him with looks of affection and trust. 'That', said General Spears admiringly, 'is the epitome of the 1917 mutinies. It is the whole story of the way you handled them.' 'You understand the meaning of my group at once,' the Marshal replied. 'Not many people do . . . I wish that group to commemorate me to the French people one day.'

General Spears went away, and his sadness was tinged with pity for a very old man. None the less, the Marshal—tired, anxious, touched with senility—had conveyed his message silently. His place was with the people. Next day General Spears told

Winston Churchill of his certainty that Pétain would never leave France.

The battle raged with an ever-increasing fury. The 'hedgehogs' were soon left deep in the enemy's new territory, and when the Germans broke through the French positions at Forges-les-Eaux, they made a gap through which several of their divisions poured. The French were driven back to the line of the Seine, and the battle was only five days old when Weygand warned Reynaud that 'a complete break-through is possible at any moment'. The enemy might use the bridgeheads on the lower Seine to turn the flank north of Paris; with his armour he might break through the defence line in Champagne; or by his treble superiority in numbers he might prevent the French from keeping a solid front on the lower Seine, the Marne and before Paris. 'Should any such eventuality arise,' Weygand wrote, 'our armies would continue to fight to the last man and the last gun. But their complete dispersal would be only a question of time.'

None escaped the confusion of lightning movement, and while Rommel drove his tanks towards Rouen passers-by raised a cheer in the belief that they were British. He was approaching Cherbourg when he took as prisoners some British officers returning innocently from a swim in the Channel. By the time Cherbourg surrendered to his few men in tanks he knew that the war with France was virtually over.

For the day on which Weygand handed his note to the Prime Minister was heavily seared with fresh disaster. In fog and mist German tanks got across the lower Seine, and by the loss of this covering position Paris was doomed to face the assault. Many thousands of her citizens sought escape along crowded roads to the west and to the south. Others waited for the ordeal, not knowing whether it would spare their homes or their lives. But Weygand decided that the defence of Paris was no longer tenable, and on his own initiative he declared her to be an open city. A few hours later Italy declared war on France.

The Government was now bound to leave Paris. 'We will fight

before Paris,' Reynaud wrote to President Roosevelt. 'We will
fight behind Paris. We will hold one of our provinces, and if we
are driven from it, we will go to North Africa and, if need be, to
our American possessions. Part of the Government has already
left Paris. I myself am on the point of joining the Armies. It will be
to intensify the struggle and not to abandon it. May I ask you,
Mr President, to explain this to your people and to tell them that
we are resolved to sacrifice ourselves in the struggles we are carrying out on behalf of all free men?'

That night Pétain slept in an inspector's room in the railway
station at Gien. Except as a prisoner he was never to see Paris
again. A million men had died on the Verdun salient and the gateway to Paris had not been pierced, but now there was nothing to
stop the enemy's tanks from clanking down the Champs-Elysées.
Pétain did not know what was in Weygand's mind. He had taken
care to avoid seeing the Commander-in-Chief alone, for he was
himself a Minister, and no longer a serving soldier. But his whole
philosophy of war taught him that the fighting man must be
machine-protected. In the Great War, as it was still known, he
had been impatient with generals who failed to realize that the loss
of the industrial towns in the north would soon create a desperate
shortage of shells. Now France would lose the industrial area of
Paris as well. The enemy held the country at its heart. Was not
the struggle bound to end in defeat? When defeat has become
inevitable, is it right to prolong by a single day the people's
sufferings?

Paul Reynaud read the last note which Weygand gave him, but
he said nothing. He no longer saw eye to eye with the Commander-in-Chief. He understood very well the significance of armoured
warfare; for, like Rommel, he had been de Gaulle's willing pupil.
But, unlike Pétain, he believed in the power of the spoken word
and the impressive gesture. He kept his faith in support from
Britain and in the immediacy of help from the United States. If
Pétain read the eleventh-hour appeal which Reynaud made to
Roosevelt, it gave him no comfort. Time, he knew, was a military

factor, and in the Great War he had waited a whole year before the help which he wanted from America came to him. In this nightmarish June the advantages of an American declaration of war might be moral; they could hardly be martial.

What mattered now was the help coming at once from the harassed British, and on the first day of the Ministers' exile from Paris Pétain drove with Admiral Darlan to meet Winston Churchill and Anthony Eden on the airfield at Briare. The general confusion caused the two British statesmen to arrive late; and meanwhile General Weygand, his patience sorely tried, waited in the Château du Muguet. It was his chance to see the Prime Ministers of France and Britain together and to make both of them realize the full dangers of the losing battle. There were things which he had to say 'for the bare truth's sake'. His retreating armies were continually shrinking. Already they had lost two-thirds of their former strength. Many had fought for six days without any relief, and wherever they halted they fell into a deep sleep. The two Prime Ministers must be told bluntly that no reserves were left; but it was not until seven in the evening that Reynaud led the Englishmen into the conference room. With him were Pétain and de Gaulle.

'The German mechanized columns get through our lines,' General Weygand announced brusquely. 'They curl round and blow up the bridges behind our troops who, when they reach them, find themselves cut off. In other cases, as the enemy aircraft can spot French troop movements unhindered, they blow up the bridges they are making from the air . . . It is a race between the exhaustion of the French and the shortness of breath of the enemy divisions. . . . There is nothing to prevent the enemy reaching Paris. We are fighting on the last line and it has been breached. . . . I am helpless. I cannot intervene, for I have no reserves. There are no reserves. It is the break-up.'

Winston Churchill listened intently to each word. He looked shocked, but he made no comment. Instead, he asked that General Georges should be summoned, and General Georges came out from the next room to make a statement as sombre as his chief's. The situation was all the more dangerous, he said, because Italy's entry into the war compelled them to send fighter squadrons to the southern front 'at the very time that our fighter force is reduced to a mere 170 or 180 machines manned by pilots who physically are in a state of exhaustion'.

For a long time Marshal Pétain had sat in the room as a silent observer. He heard Winston Churchill saying that four divisions were now in France and that a fifth would arrive about the 20th. 'If only the French Army can hold on', the Englishman added, 'it will be more like twenty or twenty-five divisions that we will send over to help you in the spring of 1941.' They were brave words, and for a while they made an impression. But Churchill had been followed by Weygand and Georges, and Pétain knew that what they said was the naked truth. Driblets of help could not check the battle. Time was too limited. France wanted all Britain's bomber strength and all her fighter strength as well.

Behind his eloquence and warmth of sympathy Churchill was a man who always put Britain first, just as the Marshal always put France first, and now Pétain listened while the Englishman explained why his country could not allow the whole of its fighter strength to be based in France. He was thinking of an imminent battle of Britain and imagining that the battle of France was merely a round in a world conflict. But to Pétain, as to nearly all other Frenchmen, the battle of France was the decisive battle. Once it was lost, Britain would be bound to submit to Hitler's will.

Churchill looked first at one Frenchman and then at another. They gave him no help. Even de Gaulle was silent. Britain's leader, however, was not in the ugly Château du Muguet to talk of defeat, and since the French had no ideas to offer, he threw out some of his own. The British, he said, could make a counter-attack near Rouen; and he recalled the state of the public mind in the spring of 1918. At that time many believed that all was lost; and they were wrong. The remark was just; but it stung the deaf Marshal into speech, and his words were bitter.

In the critical phase of the battle in 1918, Pétain replied, he had sent more than three or four divisions to the help of General Gough's Fifth Army. Within the first few days he sent twenty divisions. Later he increased their number to forty. French soldiers were now fighting without any reserves. Yet even at Verdun troops in the front line were relieved every third day. 'In those days', Pétain added tersely, 'there were sixty British divisions in the line.' He returned for a while to silence, but he was again roused to anger when he heard Churchill saying that he wanted the French to fight in Paris. 'To make Paris into a city of ruins', he retorted, 'will not affect the issue.'

There followed an argument between the two Prime Ministers on the use of Britain's air force. The French wanted far more than a few British divisions; they wanted the fullest possible air-cover. 'Were it not for the German air force', Reynaud said, 'the outcome of the present struggle would be very different.' But the bolder Reynaud made his demands the more adamant Churchill became. The air arm was the one effective weapon left to the British after the withdrawal from Dunkirk, and they would not allow it to be completely absorbed before the attack on England; for even its full use in the battle of France would not tip the scale the other way.

They were hard words, but Pétain made no comment. 'France first' or 'Britain first': here were sentiments which he understood. He would have welcomed the help which enabled the French, even now, to hurl back the enemy; but he was not assisting the British to fight a war to the last Frenchman. With silent disapproval he heard Churchill producing his own variant of a Breton redoubt, which he called an Atlantic bridgehead; and then, undaunted, the Englishman suggested that, if ever co-ordinated defence became impossible, France should at once organize guerilla bands to disrupt and harry the enemy while the British got ready to strike. The idea of guerilla warfare was too much for Pétain to accept. 'It is the complete destruction of France,' he said. His was the last word on the French side, and the meeting ended in an atmosphere of mounting gloom.

H

The reports which reached the château on the following morning offered no relief, and General Georges, whose military judgment the British trusted, told Churchill that the chances of continued resistance were slender; soon there might be no alternative to an armistice. Churchill did not argue with him. He merely said that, speaking for himself, he would continue the fight. He walked solemnly to his car. Before he entered it he turned to General Doumenc and said: 'Rest assured that, whatever happens, Britain will never abandon France.'

Left behind in the château was the troubled Marshal. Defeat on the soil of France, he believed, was a certainty, and he had been angered by Reynaud's statement that he would carry on the struggle from Africa. 'But you cannot abandon France,' he cried. To this Reynaud replied: 'Do you believe that I could govern in France with Hitler?' Now, walking through the hall, he saw General Spears. There was no further need to convey a silent message. He spoke to the British general openly.

'An armistice is inevitable,' he said, 'and it is sheer pusillanimity to shirk the issue. Whilst Ministers hesitate and think of their reputations soldiers are being killed and the land of France is being ruined. We must pay now, and pay heavily, for the anarchy we have indulged in for so long. Where now are the deputies who sought popularity by voting against any measures of re-armament? And the Popular Front, where are its leaders now that the poor deluded chaps who went about with clenched fists have nothing but clenched fists to shake at the German tanks?'

General Spears replied with vigour and urged that the French should fight in Africa.

'Africa?' said Pétain. 'What is the use of sending recruits to Africa, as Reynaud wishes? There are no rifles there to arm them with. In any case, the disorganizations of the Ministry of War is such that they could never get the men to the harbours, still less to sea, where Italian submarines would undoubtedly drown them.'

'You cannot leave us to fight alone,' the Englishman replied.

'You have left us to fight alone.'

The argument went on, but the Marshal softened his words. 'I had not meant to say it that way. Your people are doing the best they can, as we are. I am thinking of between the wars.' At last he said: 'You have no army. What could you achieve when the French Army has failed?'

'But you heard the Prime Minister?'

'Words are very fine,' Pétain answered. 'But you cannot beat Hitler with words'; and he went on to say that the British could not stand up to the Germans for more than a month. To imagine that a longer resistance was possible was a cruel self-deception.

That morning belief in the necessity of an armistice gained another important adherent; and he was the Commander-in-Chief. Fresh reports convinced him that the military situation had become hopeless. The Council of Ministers was meeting at Cangé, near Tours, in the evening, and as he had been asked to attend, he would break the news to Reynaud in the presence of his colleagues. In the afternoon he set off for Cangé, and he carried the fateful reports in his brief-case. It was the brief-case in which he had taken to the forest of Compiègne—in November, 1918—the terms of an armistice for the beaten Germans.

What he told the Ministers as they sat on each side of President Lebrun was stark and terrible. Armoured cars were making new and deep inroads, and there was no hope of reserves to take the place of exhausted troops. Without an armistice the whole of France must fall into the occupation of the enemy, and when the Army was broken there would be chaos.

Everywhere, indeed, was the confusion of movement; the circling of aeroplanes and tanks, the pitiable marches of civilians who hardly knew where they were going. Stories were legion of heroic resistance and coolness. The soldier trapped near Lille or captured at St Valéry or wounded from the air as he withdrew in agonizing weariness towards the Loire was a man beaten not by want of courage but by the nature of his unequal struggle with the machine. The nerves which should have bound him to the High Command were numbed and torn.

So, too, were the nerves which should have bound the people to their Government. The Ministers sitting with the President of the Republic knew that they were puppets. Yet they could not at once bring themselves to believe that Weygand's words were true. They began, each in turn, to give their reasons for continuing the struggle. The Germans, they said, would refuse to grant an armistice. They spoke of Churchill's determination to fight on and of the vast potentiality of help from America. They were looking, perhaps, for another miracle of the Marne; but the intruder was never to lose the initiative, and in the end the alternative to an armistice would be capitulation.

All the Ministers, save Pétain and de Gaulle, were civilian-minded. In Parliamentary debate their weapons had been phrases, which they called battle-cries. Grandiloquent words did duty for deeds. It was the military-minded who realized more speedily that an armistice is not a surrender, but a respite. It defines rights and conditions between one side and the other. The terms of an armistice can be rejected or accepted.

Such, at least, is the theory of an armistice. But the civilian-minded saw clearly that Hitler was no ordinary foe. With demonic fury he hacked at the foundations of civil liberty. Wherever his soldiers went they were followed by the Gestapo, and he would turn the demand for an armistice into a loathsome humiliation. In practice the difference between an armistice and capitulation would be negligible. Yet one Minister supported the decision which the Commander-in-Chief had reached and he was Pétain. For all the weaknesses of old age, his prestige with the people was immense. He spoke; and never again was Reynaud to command a united Cabinet.

The Prime Minister sent an urgent message to London and Churchill agreed to return. At three o'clock—on the afternoon of Thursday, June 13—President Lebrun awaited Churchill's arrival. With him were Pétain and most of the other Ministers. Weygand, too, was waiting. The meeting was likely to be heated and dramatic; the time pressed heavily. The Marshal and the Commander-in-Chief had made up their minds, but most of the others were bewildered by the need for decision. As patriots, they longed to see the struggle continued, and they resented the logic of military events. They were looking for a lead; and of all Englishmen Winston Churchill was the one who best understood the plight of France. Nearly a year beforehand he had been given a place of honour in the Champs-Élysées, so that he might see a magnificent Bastille Day parade; and many, recognizing him, gave a cheer, though he was not even a member of the British Government.

His fame was now distorted, but not destroyed, by the loss of the northern armies. If disaster fell upon British troops it was because their commanders followed the French plan, but Churchill was not upbraiding the French for a failure of military judgment; his awareness of the present was too strong. A sixth sense came to the aid in time of peril, making him as alert as the primeval man who scents danger in the forest. He could answer the defeatist and rally the perplexed. Yet more than three hours went by, and Churchill did not come.

None of the waiting Ministers knew the cause of the delay. In his pocket the Marshal had a paper on which he put methodically his argument for seeking an armistice. He would read them out, if need be, in Churchill's presence. General Weygand, too, had hard news to break to the two Prime Ministers when they arrived, for German troops were already reaching Paris. But, when at last Reynaud appeared, he was without Churchill. The British statesman, he explained, did not have time to come as far as Cangé: so he went to meet him at Tours. He was able to tell Churchill that the Government meant to continue the struggle.

The Ministers, shaken by the fall of Paris, could not hide their annoyance. They had waited impatiently to talk things over with Churchill. That was a necessary step before reaching any decision on an armistice; and Churchill had gone to the wrong meeting. Reynaud came to Cangé with a new-found confidence. He had

asked President Roosevelt to declare war, he said, and now his
colleagues must await the reply from Washington.

Pétain listened, but he was not impressed. He knew what
Roosevelt's answer would be. He had seen the American administration at work, and he knew that the right to declare war is vested
in Congress. The opinion of a democratic republic far from the
searing battlefield was not to be mobilized overnight. France's
plight was not causing the American people to go without their
sleep. At this desperate stage their help was even more chimerical
than it had been in the spring of 1917, when a declaration of war
neither altered Nivelle's crazy offensive nor checked a mutiny.
Though Churchill was on his way back to London, the moment
had come when the Marshal must read his statement.

'We all admit', he declared, 'that today the military situation is
very grave. It is such that if the French Government does not ask
for an armistice, it is to be feared that the troops, no longer listening to the voice of their chiefs, will give way to a panic which pre-
vents the Army from making the least manoeuvre . . . It is necessary to examine thoroughly the consequences which will flow
from the continuation of the struggle. If one acecpts the idea of
carrying on, thanks to the creation of a national redoubt, one
should realize that the defence of this redoubt cannot be organized
by disrupted French troops, but by fresh English divisions. Even
if this redoubt, established in a coastal region, could be organized,
in my opinion it would not constitute a guarantee of security and
would expose the Government to the temptation of giving up this
uncertain refuge.

'Now it is impossible for the Government, without emigrating
or without deserting, to quit French territory. The duty of the
Government, whatever happens, is to stay in the country under
the pain of being no longer recognized as such. To rob France
of her natural defenders at a time of general disorder is to deliver
her to the enemy: it is to kill the soul of France; it is, in conse-
quence, to make her re-birth impossible. For French renewal it is
necessary to rely fully upon the spirit of our country, which we

shall preserve by remaining where we are, rather than upon the re-conquest of our territory by allied cannons under conditions and after a period of time impossible to foresee.

'I am, therefore, of the opinion that we should not abandon French soil and should accept the suffering which will be imposed on the country and on its sons. The French Renaissance will be the fruit of this suffering. Thus the question which arises at this moment is not to know whether the French Government asks, or does not ask, for the armistice; it is to know whether it agrees to quit metropolitan France. As far as I am concerned, I declare that, whatever the Government may do, I will refuse to leave the metropolitan soil. I will remain with the French people to share their griefs and troubles.'

Reynaud had listened impatiently. He tried to dismiss the statement with a gesture of contempt. 'It is contrary to the honour of France,' he declared. Those words stung the Commander-in-Chief. 'Gentlemen,' Weygand rasped, 'honour is in those who fight rather than in those who sit in armchairs and only watch.' But Reynaud ignored the rebuke. He was playing for time. He had sent his appeal to Roosevelt and he would wait for an answer. That night the Ministers left Cangé for Bordeaux.

Pétain reached the new make-shift capital more than ever convinced that the end of the struggle was swiftly approaching. The Army's scope for action had been ripped away. The Breton redoubt was useless without the speedy arrival of British troops; and its defenders, like the soldiers retiring dispirited to the Loire, were still at the mercy of the overwhelmingly superior German air force. British troops, in their turn, would be helpless without ample artillery and air-cover. Only two courses were now open to the French. One was to ask for an armistice. The other was to capitulate.

For it was as capitulation that the two soldiers, independently of each other, interpreted Reynaud's talk of resistance renewed from North Africa. Each knew something about the greatness of the French possessions; for General Weygand had been High

Commissioner in Syria and the Marshal had waged a war in
Morocco. Each reacted sharply against the proposal to quit the
motherland. The possessions might be French, but, except for a
political artifice, they were not France. If troops in their tens of
thousands could reach Marseilles and other southern ports, where
were the ships to carry them across the Mediterranean? Could
Britain send ships to these ports in time? Politicians talked as
freely as soldiers about their honour, but they were less quarter-
master-minded.

Yet in the past victory was sometimes snatched from the hour of
defeat. France had marvelled at the coming of St Joan, and the
people now tramping on the roads had Catholicism in their bones.
Older men still talked of the battle of the Marne as though it had
been a miracle, and the legend of the angels at Mons once spread
among simple-hearted soldiers because it was believed. In actual
fact, the battle of the Marne was a shrewd grasp of time; for the
lightning phase of the first war had outrun its course, and in a fateful moment the German High Command dared to hesitate. There
had been such moments in the present battle. The deadliest tank
must halt its journey. The confusion of battle can trouble the
advancing foe as well as friend.

Meanwhile—on Friday, June 14—German troops marched
unmolested into the heart of Paris. Without a struggle she became
the beautiful diadem of Hitlerite Europe, and in her plight many
read the inextricable doom of France. Yet de Gaulle was in London busily negotiating for ships to take troops to North Africa.
That morning, too, General Alan Brooke called on Weygand to
tell him that part of a Canadian division had arrived to join those
British troops who were still in France. They would form the
nucleus of a re-instated British Expeditionary Force, and the two
generals agreed that they should be used for the defence of the
Breton redoubt. The battle still raged, and on the morrow Weygand would answer Pétain's summons to attend a Council of
Ministers in Bordeaux. By then, the Marshal's letter told him,
Roosevelt's reply would be known.

Chaos kept Weygand from reaching Bordeaux in time for the Council. He entered the Prefecture to learn that the British were no longer keeping his day-old agreement with General Brooke. London, it seemed, had decided that the battle of France was almost over. Weygand learned, too, that the Prime Minister wanted the President of the Republic to leave France together with all members of the Government, the Senate and the Chamber of Deputies. The Army was then to capitulate.

Reynaud believed that he was following sound example. Though open resistance was at an end in Norway, Holland and Belgium the Governments of those countries had put themselves beyond the enemy's reach. The King of Norway and the Queen of the Netherlands set up their courts in London. The French Government could leave France, as it had left Paris, and still find asylum on French territory. Here was a civilian solution. To Weygand it spelt safety for the politicians, dishonour for the Army, enslavement for the people.

In the evening, after the Ministers had met again, Reynaud left the Council room to tell Weygand that his wish was a command. The Government was definitely leaving France, and all troops left on the soil of the homeland must capitulate. That order Weygand flatly refused to give. He walked out of the Prefecture convinced that he would be summarily dismissed from his post. On the following morning—Saturday, June 16—the Council met again, and several Ministers were demanding Weygand's dismissal, when Camille Chautemps, Vice-President, put forward a proposal. Before leaving the country, he said, it was expedient to ask the Germans for their armistice terms. The remark shook Reynaud. Hitherto, he believed, Chautemps was on his side. When both Vice-Presidents—Chautemps and Pétain—talked of an armistice, the rift in the Cabinet was becoming serious.

Chautemps had scarcely finished speaking, however, when all eyes were riveted on the Marshal. Throughout the previous day he had sat near to the Prime Minister. His face was ashen-pale, cold and mask-like. Since reading his written plea for an armistice he had not spoken, but now he drew a document from his pocket. It was his letter of resignation. He wished to resign, he said, because of the delay in asking for an armistice. Once more the Prime Minister played for time. As the letter was addressed to him personally, he said, the resignation could not become effective until he had accepted it. Without another word Pétain put the letter back into his pocket.

This second incident was almost too much for Reynaud to endure, and he told President Lebrun that he wished to resign himself. The President begged him not to do so, for he believed that the majority of Ministers were still on his side; let him rely on the rule of the majority. That rule, Reynaud replied, worked with the Senate and the Chamber, but not with the Council of Ministers. A Government without unity could not hope to give decision and leadership. Reynaud had played for time so that his colleagues might hear Roosevelt's reply in his telegram; and the reply, as Pétain had guessed, was disappointing. It gave the assurance that 'as long as the French nation continues to defend its liberty, and in so doing the cause of democratic institutions in the world, it can reply upon receiving from the United States in ever-increasing quantities material and supplies of all kinds'. But the sting was in the next sentence: 'I know that you will understand that these declarations imply no military commitments. Congress alone can undertake such engagements.' The reply loaded the dice against Reynaud. He must now lose in the battle of wills. The majority, perhaps, were still on his side. But what of Pétain, whom the people adored? What of Weygand, whom the Council had failed to dismiss?

Perplexities multiplied, and before agreeing to release the French from their pledge never to make a separate peace, the British imposed a stern condition: the Fleet was to sail for British ports. Sunday dawned without a ray of hope. Yet Reynaud was arguing wearily with General Spears and with Sir Ronald Campbell, the British Ambassador, when the telephone rang. At the other end was de Gaulle, speaking from London. Reynaud listened and was astonished. He said that he must take down the message. Word for word, using a gold pencil, he copied the draft for a joint declaration between the French and British Governments. Their countries were to enter into 'indissoluble union'.

'The two Governments', so ran the draft statement, 'declare that France and Great Britain shall no longer be two nations, but one Franco-British Union. The constitution of the Union will provide for joint organs of defence, foreign financial and economic policies. Every citizen of France will enjoy immediately citizenship of Great Britain; every British subject will become a citizen of France . . . During the war there shall be a single War Cabinet, and all the forces of Britain and France, whether on land, sea or in the air, will be placed under its direction. It will govern from wherever it best can. The two Parliaments will be formally associated. The nations of the British Empire are already forming new armies. France will keep her available forces in the field, on the sea and in the air . . .'

Reynaud was jubilant. Here in his hand he held the clear proof that Britain meant to throw everything, even her nationhood, into the scales. The telephone rang again. This time the caller was Churchill. Without a doubt, Reynaud said, the offer would be accepted. A Cabinet meeting was about to begin, and he would tell his colleagues. He went to the meeting re-armed with courage. Churchill had suddenly equipped him to fight a new round with the defeatists. But the round was the last.

The offer had come too late. No eloquent declaration could do duty for the discarded agreement with General Brooke nor hasten the arrival of more British or Canadian soldiers in France: and the offer, if accepted, committed the French to fighting outside the homeland. What then was the use of a Franco-British Union? Whatever happened, Chautemps insisted, France must not become another British Dominion. Nor was Pétain in the least impressed. He was like a tight-fisted peasant trying hard to rescue his heritage from the storm; it was better to cling to a damaged property than to share disputed title-deeds with a neighbour.

As soon as he realized that Churchill's offer was not acceptable, Reynaud changed the subject, for the immediate issue was the renewal of the struggle from North Africa. But Pétain would not hear of it. He spoke for France, immortal and yet living always in a state of danger. For him France was the people huddled on the roadsides, the soldiers without arms. They would never forgive desertion. 'If we leave France', he said despairingly, 'we shall never find her again.'

An hour or two later Reynaud resigned, and he told President Lebrun that he should ask Pétain to form an administration. It was strange advice, for he must have known that the Marshal would not hesitate for a moment before asking for an armistice. The training which had made Pétain prepare for every emergency did not desert him in extreme old age, and as soon as the President received him he drew another document from his pocket. It was his list of the Cabinet Ministers. He read out the names, and the Commander-in-Chief who had been awaiting ignominious dismissal was now Minister of War.

The formalities were soon over. The Prime Minister spoke no words of comfort to his predecessor or to former colleagues whose fault was the patriotic longing that France should not bow her knee to a cruel invader. For each one of them it had been a time of agonizing decision. But for Marshal Pétain the tragedy of France lay far beyond the walls of an improvised Council room in Bordeaux. As Weygand said of him in a later year, 'he loves collectivities—the people, the soldier, and, above all, the peasant. But he does not love individuals, and that is why he is a difficult master to serve.' He was, moreover, in a hurry He sent a radio message to the German High Command asking for an armistice. Then he went to the microphone with his speech. He was determined to break the news to the people himself.

'Frenchmen,' he said, 'at the appeal of the President of the Republic I assume today the direction of the Government of France. Sure of the affection of our fine army, which struggles with a heroism worthy of our long military traditions against an enemy superior in numbers and in arms, sure that by its magnificent resistance it has fulfilled its duties to our allies, sure of the support of the ex-servicemen whom I have the honour to command, sure of the confidence of the entire people, I make to France the gift of my person to alleviate her sufferings.

'In these sad hours I think of the unhappy refugees who, in an extreme catastrophe, trail along our highways. I express to them my compassion and my solicitude. It is with a heavy heart that I tell you today that it is necessary to try to bring the combat to an end.

'I have sent a message this evening to the adversary asking him if he is ready to seek with us, as between soldiers, apart from the struggle and in honour the means of putting an end to the hostilities.

'May all Frenchmen group themselves round the Government over which I preside and may they endure their anguish in silence while keeping only their faith in the destiny of the homeland.'

It was eight in the evening when Reynaud resigned. Within three hours the Marshal had formed his own administration, broadcast a message to the German High Command and broken the news to the people of France. He resolved to act, as he had acted during the mutiny, with the utmost personal authority.

There remained one task to complete before the day ended, and that was to send a formal request for an armistice to the German and Italian Governments. The Marshal meant to approach the German Government through Berne and the Italian Government through the Vatican. Yet, at the very dawn of political power, he allowed a subtle change to be made in his plans. Among the fugitives from Paris was a former Prime Minister, now staying with Adrien Marquet, Mayor of Bordeaux and a close personal friend. So long as Reynaud was in office the fugitive kept himself a little aloof. He dined alone and observed a silence strange to his nature.

The Mayor's friend knew when to pass from silence to action. As soon as he heard that Marshal Pétain wished to approach Berlin through Berne, he suggested the alternative that the Spanish Ambassador, Señor de Lequeries, should be asked to transmit the message through Madrid. It was ingratiating advice, and Pierre Laval decided that he need sit on the fence no longer. The dream of treating a Marshal of France like a marionette might come true.

CHAPTER SEVEN

HEAD OF THE STATE

MARSHAL PÉTAIN put a fleshless hand to the wheel when the ship of State was near wreckage. Even before he asked for an armistice, the British had begun to withdraw their troops from France, and within two days sixty thousand soldiers sailed from Brest and Saint-Nazaire for English ports. Yet Pétain did not want to break the Entente, and Weygand's first act as Minister of War had been to transfer to Britain's account all the orders for war material which France gave to the United States. In Bordeaux, on June 19, Admiral Darlan, the new Minister of Marine, met A. V. Alexander, First Lord of the Admiralty, and Admiral Sir Dudley Pound, and he gave the two Englishmen his word that the Fleet would never pass to the Germans. He also put officers under secret orders to sink their ships if German troops should take possession of the ports in which they lay at anchor.

After this meeting Admiral Darlan called on the Marshal, whom he found talking with Reynaud. Pétain was urging his predecessor to sink political differences and, in the hour of peril, to go to Washington as Ambassador. Reynaud listened while the Admiral described his encounter with the two Englishmen and their reactions to his promise. Like many thousands of Frenchmen, the former Prime Minister was still at a loss to decide where his duty lay, and he did not at once reject Pétain's plea.

Now France was more than ever at the mercy of her foe, for Pétain's broadcast address took away the last hope of a change in military fortune. Behind the Loire the message flashed from one group of exhausted troops to the other that all was over.

Defeat had come, and no heart was left for the forlorn fighting.

Out of the darkness a voice had spoken. On June 18, as the last ship was bringing back British troops from France, a French officer went to the microphone in London and called on his countrymen to resist. 'Nothing is lost for France,' he declared. 'The same means that defeated us can one day bring us victory. For France is not alone . . . I, General de Gaulle, at present in London, request all French officers and men who are now, or who may soon find themselves, in British territory, with or without arms: I request all engineers and skilled workers in the armaments industries who are now, or may soon find themselves, in British territory, to get in touch with me. Whatever happens the flame of French resistance must not, and will not, go out.'

These words, though brave and strong, could not wipe out the Marshal's piteous statement, and if the stragglers beyond the Loire heard de Gaulle's appeal, they ignored it. To men in the ranks of a broken regiment resistance from London seemed even more pointless than resistance from North Africa, and within a matter of weeks the invincible foe must sweep across the Channel, leaving the people of France as defenceless as the Poles. Now that the call for an armistice had been made, the people longed to see the end of the fighting. Six millions of them were on the roads of conquered France. They were homeless and hungry.

The foe, while promptly acknowledging the request for an armistice, delayed its formalities, and each passing day increased the danger that he would see his own disadvantage in allowing an armistice to be signed. By the sheer weight of metal, armour and men he must soon reach the shore of the Mediterranean and the footholds of the Pyrenees. Then capitulation would be inevitable and the way would open to the conquest of North Africa. Hitler would rule the Mediterranean and add a continent to his dominions.

Vanity, however, warped his judgment. As conquerer, he gloried in reversing the military decision of 1918. He remembered the railway dining-car in which Foch and Weygand watched the signing of an armistice. He would remove the car from its stand in the courtyard of the Invalides and bring it back to the railway siding at Rethondes in the forest of Compiègne. There silently he would watch the humiliated French signing a new armistice. It would be his 'reparative act of justice'. He was in a hurry to show himself as master of Europe.

On June 21, General Huitzinger and the other plenipotentiaries arrived at Tours. Without warning German officers took them to Rethondes, where an organized crowd awaited them. Between batteries of cameras and to the strains of triumphal music they walked to the dining-car. Hitler entered, and he spoke not a word. General Keitel snapped out a declaration: 'France, after resisting heroically and fighting without ceasing a number of bloody battles, has been defeated and is now prostrate. In these circumstances Germany will not impose upon so brave an enemy conditions of a humiliating character. The conditions she offers are intended, in the first place, to prevent any recurrence of hostilities; in the second place, to enable Germany to carry on without hindrance the war against Britain, this continuance of the struggle being forced on Germany by that country; and, in the third place, to ensure the establishment of a new peace under which the injustice done to Germany in the past will be put right.'

Not once did Hitler break his silence; but he was not listening to Keitel. Panther-like he paced up and down the dining-car, and the Frenchmen were made aware of his demonic strength of purpose. He towered above them, for at that moment he corrected what he believed to be an historic wrong. Silence took away vulgarity.

Over a telephone General Huitzinger slowly read out the terms of the armistice to General Weygand. Right through the night Pétain discussed them with his Cabinet. He drew up amendments, most of which the Germans rejected. In the afternoon the Cabinet agreed that the terms must be accepted. Word was sent to General Huitzinger, and after they had signed the document the plenipotentiaries left Compiègne for Rome. On the 25th the Marshal

I

went to the microphone and told the people that at last the armistice had come into force. 'Wars are won,' he said, 'not with gold and raw materials, but with troops, supplies and the way they are used, and in these the Germans had a crushing superiority.' This crushing superiority, however, was less evident to the defenders of the Maginot Line than to the troops who had been driven back from the Seine; and many went on resisting until, on the 26th, the German High Command declared that unless their resistance ended at once the whole country would be occupied. At midnight fighting ceased on all fronts in France.

This was the only armistice which Hitler ever authorized, and the terms were stiff. The Germans would occupy Northern France as well as the whole Atlantic border to a depth of thirty kilometres. They would leave unoccupied a large zone flanked by the Mediterranean coast, and within this unoccupied zone the French were allowed to keep an Army one hundred thousand strong. Their possessions overseas were to be left to them untouched, and the Fleet was ordered to remain within the ports.

France, humiliated in spite of Keitel's words, had a few cards left to play. The occupied zone included Paris, the Channel and Atlantic ports and all the industrial areas save Lyons and Marseilles. Yet the overseas possessions were intact, and so was the Fleet. Apart from the one hundred thousand soldiers allowed in the unoccupied zone, there was nearly twice that number of troops in Africa. Armistice, it was clear, paid a better dividend than capitulation. The President of the Republic, the Council of Ministers, the Senate and the Chamber of Deputies stayed on the soil of France. A few deputies like Edouard Daladier might have embarked in the *Massilia* to carry on a political resistance from Algiers. General de Gaulle might have reached London as a lone adventurer lacking authority; but the Third Republic was not yet formally destroyed. Unlike Poland or Holland, beaten France was not condemned to rule by a Gauleiter.

But the thoughts of the people were far from politics. Their first response to the armistice had been relief and thankfulness.

Their second was penitence. Defeat was akin to punishment. The moment the armistice came into force the Marshal attended a crowded service in the cathedral of Bordeaux, and he had the look of a dedicated man. The people needed a leader to reflect their suffering, their grief, their dignity. 'I make to France the gift of my person to alleviate her sufferings.' With those words the hero took on the guilt of the whole nation. Sharing the people's guilt as well as their sufferings, he would lead them. Beaten and prostrate, the people would not have looked at a politician. The Third Republic had died in their hearts.

The problems before the aged leader were desperate. For many days to come the roads would be choked with civilians trying to get back to their homes. They must be fed, clothed, sheltered. Many would be crippled in their work by a zonal frontier drawn through the heart of the country and cutting off the Atlantic coast. Mothers were separated from their children, and the encirclement of whole divisions had made many wives penniless. For a long time it would be difficult even to assess the numbers of the killed and the wounded. To restore the afflicted to their homes, to plan for the release of untold thousands of prisoners-of-war, to get the people working again for the common good: these were tasks not one whit less formidable than the defence of Verdun or the quelling of a mutiny.

Great age refines, but it does not change, a man's character. The Marshal was still more at ease with sergeants and poilus than with the highest-ranking officers. Yet his sympathy with the peasant had rarely made him impatient with the hierarchic principle; he objected if it became impersonal. He was more paternal than democratic. In his first report on the mutiny he had written: 'From the strict military point of view the army has only one end—victory. It has only one virtue—discipline.' Now the end for which he worked was salvation; the virtue which he extolled was still discipline; and he joined millions of his own countrymen in seeking the consolations of religion.

There was, however, no complete abasement. Armistice was not surrender. The enemy, though in actual possession of half France as well as Paris, might be worn down by the hardest war of attrition ever fought. Verdun and the mutiny were back like a two-headed monster to plague the ancient hero. He called for tears, sacrifice, work. A soldier chary of words suddenly spoke with accents more like those of Charles Maurras. Yet he was working for France in his relentless, piecemeal way: prodding, yielding, never wasting a blow. He had not lost his long patience.

Nor had he forgotten his meeting with Herbert Hoover in the White House. The simple pattern of the presidential office in America still made its strong appeal. As in the days of the mutiny, the Marshal wanted the fullest personal authority; and now he would bring to an end the rapid, ever-weakening succession of Prime Ministers. Vanity mingled with the sacrificial resolve to save France, and Pierre Laval, exploiter of human fraility, seeing where the Marshal's moral armour was thin, got ready to take away the Third Republic and to bring the institutions of France into line with those of her authoritarian conquerors. He would turn the Marshal into a figurehead, and whether or not his own office was that of Prime Minister he would pull the strings.

He played on the old man's prejudices. The obvious seat for a Government in unoccupied France was the once thriving city of Lyons, but Pétain did not want to go there because its Mayor and most influential citizen was Herriot. Obligingly Laval suggested Clermont-Ferrand, where he had substantial property. Its accommodation, however, was too restricted, and Pétain forsook the town for the relaxing spa of Vichy, where several hotels were at once requisitioned. In all France there was hardly a place more remote from the opinions and agitations of the people.

One of Pétain's first tasks in Vichy was to summon members of the Senate and the Chamber. Some were already trapped in the *Massilia*, and others were stranded in occupied France. Yet two-thirds of the Senators and deputies managed to reach Vichy, and on July 9 they met separately in the Casino. They came to pronounce the demise of the Third Republic, but many were frankly confused about the steps to be taken. Unlike Laval, they did not yet know the full answer. As a first step, Senate and Chamber passed by overwhelming majorities an identical motion that 'there is reason to revise the constitutional laws'.

Most deputies, led by Joseph Paul-Boncour, favoured a proposal to suspend the constitution of 1875 for the duration of the war and to authorize the Marshal to govern by decree, but Laval complained that this was not daring enough. 'Since parliamentary democracy chose to fight against Nazism and Fascism,' he said, 'it must disappear. A new regime, audacious, authoritarian, social and national, must be substituted for it'; and he put forward a counter-proposal to grant 'to the government of the Republic full power to promulgate the new constitution of the French State'.

The proposal looked innocent, and at first Paul-Boncour and his friends were ready to back it so long as the new constitution was afterwards ratified 'by the National Assembly which drafted it'. 'By the nation rather than by the National Assembly,' Laval replied. He was thinking of the plebiscites used first by Napoleon III and now by Hitler; and when the Senate and the Chamber met jointly as the National Assembly, he was its skilful master. By changing the normal procedure he got his own counter-proposal put to the vote before Paul-Boncour's motion, and it was passed by 569 votes to 80. In their confusion Senators and deputies whispered that they had been tricked. France, they said, was suddenly submitted to an unlawful dictatorship. An adroit blow had killed the Third Republic. Yet five out of every six participating members of the National Assembly approved the death certificate, and before they walked out of the Casino they gave the Marshal his authority to promulgate a new constitution which 'will guarantee the rights of work, family and native country'. Next day they read: 'We, Philippe Pétain, Marshal of France, by authority of the Constitutional law of July 10, declare that we assume the functions of the Head of the French State . . . ' So began the first constitutional act of the new regime.

The second act gave Pétain the command of the armed forces

and made him in outward form a dictator, save that 'he shall not
have power to declare war without the previous assent of the
Legislative Assemblies'. The third act decreed that the Senate and
the Chamber, while continuing to exist, should be adjourned until
further notice and convened only at the summons of the Head of
the State. A day later there appeared the fourth act, and it made
Laval deputy to the Head of the State.

Pétain was keeping one eye on Hitler and the other on Roosevelt. Like the Fuehrer, he donned the trappings of a personal ruler
who had no need of legislators; like the President of the United
States, he was Commander-in-Chief. He put the Legislature out
of sight while explicitly renouncing his right to go to war without
its consent. Here was his curb to any demand by Hitler that he
should make war on Britain. Here, too, was a tribute to the American Congress, in which the right to declare war is vested. It was
also, perhaps a shrewd thrust at Reynaud for his belief that a direct
appeal to her President could bring America at once into the war.

President Roosevelt and the State Department in Washington
were not unfriendly to the new regime. The American Embassy
was soon installed in Vichy, and so were the Embassies and legations of nearly all the other neutral Powers; and as he read selected letters of gratitude—many thousands, he was assured,
were coming from prisoners-of-war—the Marshal felt more than
ever confident that his country had been spared the fate of Poland.

Yet the Entente with the British was torn asunder, and Pétain
expressed dismay when their Ambassador, Sir Ronald Campbell,
was recalled from Bordeaux. That was the first unmistakable sign
that France must fall a victim to Britain's blockade of Hitler's
Europe. The armistice was barely ten days old when the British
raided French ships sheltering in the roads of Mers-el-Kebir. Fourteen hundred French officers and men lay dead. It was a cruel
blow, but on July 14, the first Bastille Day of defeat, Churchill
broadcast an assurance that ships in Toulon and other French
ports would be left alone, so long as they made no attempts to
return to ports controlled by Germans or Italians.

A full year had gone by since Churchill attended the military parade in the Champs-Élysées, and more than half the soldiers who marched past him were now prisoners. The spirit of the revolution was smothered by penitential renouncement, and already workmen were erasing the slogan of 'Liberty, Equality, Fraternity' from the public buildings. A stunned people were denying their own nature. Many pretended to be resigned, but the brave were watchful.

Pétain arranged his Cabinet as a general arranges his staff. Weygand was his link with the broken Army and Darlan his link with a Navy which had become an important diplomatic asset. Weygand thought and acted always as a soldier. It was his tragedy to be called to supreme command from distant Syria when he was ten years too old to stand the strain and when it was already too late for any general, short of a master of tank-aeroplane warfare, to stem the German onrush. He remained convinced that he had not pressed the need for an armistice a moment too soon. While he felt bitterly the reversal of military fortune, he spared no effort after the armistice to wrench order out of chaos, and he was quick to organize the light-armed troops allowed in the unoccupied zone.

He gave a wholehearted loyalty to Pétain, though there was little affinity of temperament between them. He often found the older man forbidding in manner and lacking the ebullience and quick sympathies of Foch. He feared the intrigues with which some Ministers were already surrounding him. They ought to have sunk their rivalries and trivial ambitions in the common task of deceiving the foe. For to the soldier's mind the state of armistice was never permanent, and whenever a Minister spoke of collaboration, Weygand retorted as sharply as he had done in Cangé and Bordeaux.

Darlan, too, gave loyalty to Pétain, but it was of a different order. What personal sympathy he may have had with the Head of the State was born of the days when, as an Army engineer, he fought at Verdun, and he went back to the Navy anxious to work for a closer cohesion between the services. He belonged to a dis-

ciplined, unimaginative world, and his thoughts were often nar-
rowly conditioned by the group in which he moved. The new war
with Germany found the Fleet alert and active. Its submarines
claimed many triumphs, and while a 'phoney war' on land rotted
away the defensive spirit, the seas had become a graveyard for
sailors killed on active service. The armistice was a deep humiliation to the Fleet determined to prove its mettle. Darlan had given
his word that the Fleet would never pass to the Germans, and the
raid on Mers-el-Kebir was like a crowning insult. Neither he nor
Weygand wanted to speak gently of yesterday's ally.

Darlan, like Weygand, left politics alone. If he impressed the
Nazi leaders whom he was bound to meet it was not because he
shared their politics, but because he had long moved among men
who gave and received orders. His was the service mind, and
whom he served was France. He might hate alike the British and
the Germans, but he kept personal feelings under control. The
armistice, he saw clearly, left France some measure of sovereignty;
its conditions kept open the Mediterranean and enabled the British
to feed Malta and to send their divisions to Libya. Though the
armistice stipulated that naval ships must remain in harbour, Darlan soon won from the jubilant Germans the concession that the
ships in Brest should proceed unmolested to Toulon. He was less
human than Pétain and less masterly in argument than Weygand,
but he knew how to exploit the few advantages which France in
her defeat still possessed. He admired Napoleon and circumstances
compelled him, like Pétain, to play Richelieu.

The staff-minded Marshal regarded the chief members of his
administration as a triumvirate. Weygand and Darlan were the
service leaders; the political member had to be Laval. Petain never
liked him. From the moment Laval succeeded the murdered
Barthou at the Quai d'Orsay Pétain lost the desire to stay in the
Doumergue Ministry. Yet, even as he noted the cunning and slick-
ness of his mind, he fancied that Laval was at heart a patriot. He
had watched the way in which, as Foreign Minister, he evaded the
actual ratification of his pact with the Soviet Union. He saw

how skilfully he persuaded Samuel Hoare, his opposite number in London, to bedevil the Geneva policy of sanctions against Italy. Barthou might win Pétain to a wider view of France's responsibilities in Europe, but in the end the peasant's outlook dragged him back. The soil of France came first. Her sons should not be committed to adventures abroad. She needed allies, not potential foes. She was Italy's neighbour, and not the world's knight-errant.

If only at the core of his nature Laval possessed a provincial's knotty integrity he might yet atone for a lack of outward principle. Nimble wits could trip up the Nazis and frustrate their methodical plans; but Laval was no less ambitious for himself than for France. His background was as shabby as Hitler's or Stalin's, and he, too, found compensation in the belief that he was born to wield power. 'It's good for France to be working with the victors,' Rommel wrote after the armistice. 'The peace terms will be so much the more lenient for her.' Laval would have agreed with Rommel. He disliked Britain and admired Fascist Italy. The ease with which he used to win his way in the lobbies of the Chamber merely heightened his contempt for parliamentary methods. Bargaining, cajoling, place-hunting with one's own countrymen became wearisome in the end. It was even tedious to be persuasive with the Marshal, who could be so strangely strait-laced, suspicious and obdurate. It was better to work for some improbable and dazzling end. Ribbentrop and Molotov had brought Germany and Russia together. Laval would bring Germany and France together. His country would join the league of the dictators: Hitler, Mussolini, Stalin, and one day Laval. The new Concert of Europe would have harmony.

At the moment no one had a hope of displacing Pétain as the spokesman of France. 'I am not a dictator,' the old man insisted. 'I am not a Caesar. I do not want to become one.' He was doing what he thought best for France, and he scarcely advanced beyond the father-principle. He was trying to set things right with the minimum of fuss and the minimum of words. Coldly he watched the foe. Laval regarded the foe as tomorrow's friend: treacherous and uncertain, like all other friends whom he knew in politics. A political philosophy could not be reared on the father-principle alone. Laval was ready for the paraphernalia of the Corporative State, so long as he was king-maker.

He was, indeed, more than king-maker. His subtle mastery over the National Assembly on July 10 enabled Pétain to become Head of the State and left for himself the powerful position of deputy or head of the administration. By this stratagem he ousted the Marshal from his position as Prime Minister. Laval had been Prime Minister himself under the Third Republic, but never before had he wielded power without fear of reactions and criticisms in the Chamber and the newspapers. He left Pétain his glory, while pursuing his own course of collaboration with, not strict neutrality towards, Germany.

Here he was helped by the line separating one zone from the other. Vichy was not Paris, where Otto Abetz represented the civil authority of Germany and where France herself was represented by an Ambassador. This line of demarcation cut off one member of a family from another. It could not be crossed without tedious formalities of permission, and it was a barrier even to the circulation of newspapers. The one Frenchman who crossed it freely and frequently was Laval. He noted how insidiously the line was setting one part of France against another, Paris against Vichy; but, whatever happened, he was not forsaking the goal of collaboration. The day was over for ever, so he believed, when the Germans and the French wasted their blood in a fratricidal struggle no better than civil war. He saw the red dawn of united Europe, and Pétain soon realized that he was moving out of step. The deputy was going beyond his chief, and, perhaps, in the wrong direction. The Marshal said nothing. He became more distant and majestic.

He had other things to worry him. He guessed that all too soon Hitler would see his mistake in granting an armistice; and on August 4 Paul Baudouin, his first choice as Foreign Minister, insisted on seeing him alone. The Germans were in a bad mood, Baudouin said. Within seven days an army detachment might arrive in Vichy to put an end to a Government that was not sufficiently docile. The Head of the State must be prepared.

'But what do you want me to do?' Pétain asked.

'You must have an aeroplane always ready to take you away to Algiers.'

'I have already thought about it,' Pétain replied. 'In no case will I leave France. I will let myself be taken prisoner, and you will be taken prisoner with me. Someone must always be ready to escape to Algiers. That person can only be the chief of the Fleet. Can you summon him? Come this evening at seven o'clock. You will find Admiral Darlan in my study.'

The interview between the three men lasted for an hour. At first Darlan was reluctant and silent. Then he agreed that if the Germans descended on Vichy or if the Marshal found that he could no longer govern with independence, he would do all he could to reach North Africa and to govern in the Marshal's name. He would order the Fleet to sail for North Africa. Baudouin wanted Pétain to put his signature to this order, but he refused.

'I don't want to put pen to paper,' he said, 'but you must consider my order as binding. I will not go back on this decision. Meanwhile it is well that this matter should be left strictly between the three of us. No one else should know about it.'

Another worry was the attitude of General de Gaulle. The London broadcast of June 18 was a deliberate act of defiance, and Pétain gave orders that the offender should be tried contumaciously. Yet each passing day showed that de Gaulle might have assessed aright the disaster in the field. France had lost a battle, but not a war. The British were not even thinking of an armistice. They expected an invasion, and they would fight on their own soil. Their terrible danger was not aggravated by a dark hereditary fear.

This stubbornness of attitude found an answering chord in many French minds. Pétain knew enough about the possibilities of air-warfare firmly to decide that the Germans had lost the battle of Britain and that their defeat must involve drastic changes of plan. Events might prove that Weygand was right when he talked of an armistice as though it were a pause or a mere suspension of hostilities. If Laval worked surreptitiously for a league of dictators it was because he did not understand the full nature of war. The armistice in France had magnified the resolution of the people in Britain, and neutral America was swiftly piling up her armaments. Guns, tanks, aeroplanes, a gigantic wealth of steel and armour might yet frustrate the Germans, though nearly all the industrial areas of France were now added to Hitler's dominions. In the meantime Pétain would be neutral. He would adhere strictly to the terms of the armistice, using them as the yardstick for determining France's present rights.

Nor was he alone in foreseeing a long, painfully developing world war. Others were working out its logistics. The French mind began to display its natural restlessness and curiosity. Young soldiers and airmen who had escaped capture longed to show that they were far from cowardly. Inactivity tortured the men of the Fleet in home ports. Secretively the legend of de Gaulle was taking root. Wars of attrition, military or political, are outwardly inglorious, and many were the survivors of Verdun who rejoiced when Nivelle pointed a quick way to seeming victory. Nivelle failed ignominiously, and Pétain took his place as Commander-in-Chief. The way of attrition continued; but Foch, compelled by circumstances to accept Pétain's laborious methods, transcended them for the final offensive. Foch and Pétain had been necessary to France in 1918. Pétain and de Gaulle, perhaps, were necessary to France in 1940. She needed a double insurance, and each was a soldier. Only a soldier would have met the needs of this hour. The people, while silently questioning, kept faith in the Marshal of France. Their will gave Vichy its legitimacy. 'Follow me,' Pétain said. 'Do not go beyond me.'

He asked for obedience because he could not tell the people all that was in his mind. For, distinct from their will and over-arching it, was the will of the conqueror. His will was the effective law.

Time and again he defied the conditions of the armistice. He took back Alsace-Lorraine. He administered the Pas de Calais, in which Pétain was born, as though it formed part of his Belgian satrapy. The Marshal protested against both actions, and each time his words went unheeded in Berlin. From Vichy he might issue decrees binding on all that remained of France, but throughout the occupied zone the conqueror's needs and ordinances had explicit priority. The fighting was over, but the foe kept his initiative. France had carefully to husband the little strength still left to her.

That was true, too, of the Marshal. The strain of events told heavily upon him. Sustained work and attention were sometimes difficult. Without an increasing delegation of authority the old man could not have coped with the tasks which lay nearest to his desires: to comfort the people by moving among them; to get civilians back to their homes and to their work; to secure the release of the prisoners; to watch the foe. Watchfulness had formed an essential part of his own military training. He knew, as a soldier, the importance of reading the foe's mind, forestalling his moves and, fox-like, sending him off on a wrong scent. He was still reading the old foe's mind when, as an instrument of Poincaré's policy, French troops entered the Ruhr. There he saw passive resistance holding its own against military power. It was hidden war waged with implacable coldness.

Passive resistance might soon become the weapon of saving France. She was not without resources. She had her territories overseas and the Fleet. She had a people capable of recovering their confidence. She wanted leadership disciplined, as in actual war, with a long patience. To Laval and to little-known minions were delegated more authority and power than a personal ruler in the prime of life would have dared to cede, but Pétain reserved ebbing strength for a few imperative ends. He had to be reticent and untrusting. The foe must never suspect the motives of beaten France.

Above all, Pétain had to be reticent with his Ministers. He knew secrets which he dared not share with them. Late in September,

1940, for instance, two Japanese delegates had arrived in Berlin to sign a Pact of Steel with Germany and Italy. After the ceremony Hitler talked to them openly about the next stage of the war. He planned to take Gibraltar, to occupy the ports and other areas of French North Africa and thus to close the Mediterranean to the British. He would advance upon Suez, persuade the Turks to make common cause with him and then hurl his forces against Russia. Twenty German divisions were already stationed in the south-west corner of occupied France. Soon he was going himself, Hitler said, to the Spanish frontier to meet General Franco. He would offer the Caudillo a firm alliance and ask that the twenty divisions should pass through Spain to storm Gibraltar from the land.

With the delegates was Renzo Sawada, who had known Paris since the days of the Peace Conference and was now Japanese Ambassador in Vichy. He realized that if Hitler intended to seize the ports of French North Africa, he was ready to defy his armistice with France, and incautiously he passed on the news to Colonel René Fonck. Colonel Fonck asked to see the Marshal alone. Pétain, realizing that there was no time to waste, sent for the Spanish Ambassador, Señor de Lequerica, and begged him to go at once to Madrid. He was to tell the Caudillo that if Spain refused to allow passage to the German troops France, on her part, would resist any attempt to change the conditions of the armistice. Within four days Señor de Lequerica was back in Vichy. He brought an assurance from General Franco that if France showed firmness with Hitler, Spain would yield nothing.

Once he was sure of his ground, Pétain approached Goering with a request to meet Hitler, whose train would pass through the unoccupied zone on its way back from Hendaye. Hitler readily agreed. He would talk with Marshal Pétain at Montoire on the evening of October 24, the day after his meeting with General Franco. He had, however, no intention of meeting Pétain unprepared. On October 20, Abetz, the German Ambassador in Paris, told Laval that Ribbentrop had come to France and that he was to meet him. Meanwhile he was to let no one know of the meeting, except the Marshal.

Two days later Laval left Paris with Abetz. They drove towards Rambouillet. and Abetz pretended not to know where the meeting would take place. 'We are going first to Tours and from there we will be directed to von Ribbentrop.' By the evening they reached Montoire, where the train taking Hitler to Hendaye drew into the station. Ribbentrop, indeed, was present: but it was Hitler whom Laval had been brought to see. The Fuehrer wanted to sum up a man whose career baffled him. As Laval was not a Minister when the French sued for an armistice, he could be the first of Vichy's leaders to repudiate it. How far was he to be trusted? But when Hitler spoke of 'collaboration', Laval promised to give it with a whole heart.

The train took the Fuehrer on to Hendaye, and he seemed to be well pleased with the encounter. Like Laval, he knew nothing about Pétain's surreptitious contact with General Franco. He would go back to Berlin with a double triumph. Hendaye and Montoire together would convince the world that almost the whole of Latin Europe was now hitched to the Nazi chariot.

Hitler set out to woo, and he believed that he had a special advantage. Only a few days beforehand, on October 18, General Franco had dismissed the Foreign Minister and replaced him with Serrano Suner, whom the Germans regarded as a friend. Unknown to Hitler, however, the Caudillo had carefully chosen October 25, two days after the meeting in Hendaye, as the date when Suner's appointment became effective.

Thus he was forearmed when he came face to face with the Fuehrer and heard him offering to Spain the coveted prize of Gibraltar. He feigned astonishment and gratitude, but he gave nothing away. He treated the restoration of Gibraltar as part of Spain's long-term policy. Gibraltar was hers by right, and one day her flag would fly above the citadel. She could afford to wait. There was no need, therefore, for Spain to impair her own sovereignty by allowing passage to the troops even of an ally and a friend, in whose cause she had become a co-belligerent. When Hitler won his inevitable victory, the British intruders would leave Gibraltar without a struggle. The Spanish people would then willingly acknowledge the debt which they owed to the German victor.

Next evening Hitler was back at Montoire. On the platform, where Laval had been taken by surprise, there stood the kingly and resplendant figure of the Marshal of France. He told Hitler that France was ready to give Germany all the economic collaboration which she needed. He wanted friendship and understanding to take the place of distrust and fear, and he was eager to discuss in principle the fullest harmony with the ancient foe. Yet in his own mind he had not the slightest intention of yielding an inch over the armistice terms; and Hitler, baulked of his march on Gibraltar, was in no position to press for bases in North Africa. Expansively the Fuehrer asked the Marshal if there was anything that he wished him to do, and Pétain begged for the release of General Laure, an officer who stood close to him and was completing his biography.

The Marshal saw at once the weakness of a former corporal who loved flattery. He shook hands before a battery of cameras, and thus he gave propaganda its fateful chance to convert the meeting at Montoire into an avowed desertion to the enemy. But Pétain thought that the handshake was a mere touch of the fingers, and he returned to Vichy well pleased with his deception. 'Things have gone very well, Fonck,' he said. 'But, whatever happens, don't breathe a word. They are quite capable of putting us both to death.' In private talk Pétain maintained that his discussion with Hitler was no more than a survey of the horizon. 'Tell the Duce', Ribbentrop wrote to Ciano, 'nothing of importance happened at Montoire.'

Pétain's fear of a German footing in French North Africa was fully shared by Weygand. For six weeks he had sat in the Council of Ministers, where he often upbraided Laval for his eagerness to make policy pro-German, and after a stormy session Pétain coldly relieved him of his post as Minister of War. Almost at once, however, he asked him to go to Africa as Commander-in-Chief and Delegate General. Laval, denied a military mind, imagined that Pétain gave the general a sop to injured pride. Weygand reached French North Africa impatient to put its defences in good order. A letter which the Marshal wrote him on November 9 was re-assuring.

'You were right', Pétain stated, 'in not replying to the letters from Winston Churchill and Lord Halifax and in confining yourself to acknowledgments. I, too, have been the object of numerous questions on the part of Winston Churchill and Lord Halifax, who are curious to know the object of my conversations with Hitler. I have been able to assure them—for it was the truth—that there was a question merely of a collaboration of principle. No other modality had been envisaged. In this interview I confined myself to asking for an improvement in the condition of the prisoners, in food supplies, in communications between the two zones and the suppression of the demarcation line, etc. It is probable that one day "collaboration" will quieten down. I assure you that it rests only on considerations of economic order or the defence of our African empire and is free from any idea of aggression against England. On this score I am determined to link myself neither with the Italians nor with the Germans.

'Admiral Platon is the bearer of all information likely to interest you. That the English dare to ask you to associate yourself in the work of de Gaulle shows that they are very trivial in their affairs or scarcely intelligent . . . Professor Rougier has been announced to me, but I have not yet seen him. He is considered here to be an English agent. You were quite right to insist that no one is authorized to use our air and sea bases.'

Whatever Pétain thought of English intelligence, he was silently seeking a stronger contact with the old ally across the Channel. The raid on Mers-el-Kebir had been a blow in the fog of uncertainty and disaster. The friends of yesterday were feeling their way back to the familiar landmarks, and Pétain knew more about the talks which Professor Rougier had with Churchill and Eden than he admitted in his letter to Weygand.

Nor was Professor Rougier Vichy's only link with London. On December 4 Professor Jacques Chevalier, of Grenoble University, had an unexpected visitor. He was Pierre Dupuy, Canadian Minister in Vichy, and he brought a personal message from Lord Halifax. Between Lord Halifax and Jacques Chevalier, known to many English readers as an interpreter of Bergson's philosophy, was a friendship stretching back to their undergraduate days in Oxford, and the Frenchman had often stayed at Hickleton, the Yorkshire home of Lord Halifax's father, the Anglo-Catholic spokesman. In the first World War he had been a liaison officer with the British, and in the years of peace he had worked for a closer understanding between the two countries.

Pierre Dupuy brought the message by word of mouth, and Chevalier wrote it down. The message admitted that the British were in a delicate situation. They must move warily and maintain 'a state of artificial tension' with the French; for the Germans would at once retaliate if they had an inkling of any Anglo-French undertaking. 'You have two lungs: the colonies and the Navy. If the Germans got the upper hand you would be weakened.' Lord Halifax asked that the French should guard their Fleet and their colonies and yet abstain from attacking those colonies which kept up the struggle by the side of the British.

As soon as Pétain got back to Vichy from Marseilles he received Professor Chevalier and studied the message sentence by sentence. He made a few alterations in phrasing and in substance. He wanted 'a state of artificial tension' to be changed into 'a state of artificial coldness', and he asked that the British radio should not interfere in the internal affairs of France. A day later he talked with Chevalier and Dupuy together, and he learned how French ships on their way to Dakar would pass through the Straits of Gibraltar with British navicerts.

Now he had a stronger hand, but Hitler was still France's master. If the Fuehrer fell under the Marshal's spell at Montoire, vanity would not permit the charm to last. He was about to make a gesture to the French people which, he believed, might dwarf Pétain's prestige. He was lord of Paris as well as Vienna, and he gave orders that the body of Napoleon's son, the short-lived Duke of Reichstadt, should be brought from the church of the Capuchins in Vienna and placed, like his father's, beneath the Dome of the Invalides. For more than a century the French had wanted to see the unhappy youth restored, though in death, to his dignities as King of Rome. The re-burial would be marked with sombre splendour, and Hitler would attend the ceremony. It would be his first gesture of friendship to the citizens of Paris.

Laval was in Paris when, on December 12, Abetz told him what Hitler wished to do. The ceremony would take place in two days' time, and Hitler asked that Marshal Pétain should be present. Laval protested that the invitation had come at too short a notice; the weather was cold and the Marshal old. There was no time in which to heat a residence suitable for the Head of the State. It was the Fuehrer's habit, the Ambassador replied, to make swift decisions. Laval got in touch with Vichy, and the men around Pétain complained that the shortness of notice was a discourtesy; the Marshal himself would fix the date of the ceremony. But Laval, realizing the temper of the Germans in Paris, decided to go to Vichy himself. He arrived at lunch-time on the 13th, and he found that the Marshal was not at all unwilling to accept Hitler's invitation. Indeed, he approved a letter, telling Hitler that he would go to Paris, and the Hotel Matignon was made ready for his use. By following the King of Rome to a new grave near his father's, the Marshal of France would pay tribute to Napoleon, not to Hitler.

He reckoned without General Weygand, whom the affairs of North Africa had brought suddenly to Vichy. Weygand was greatly distressed by Pétain's acceptance. The dining-car in which the two armistices were signed was back on its stand in the courtyard of the Invalides, and the shaking of dead bones was just as much a sign of danger as the shifting of museum pieces. If the Germans showed an outward deference to Marshal Pétain as Head of the State, they were still showing an outward deference to President Hacha in Prague, though they had once cruelly humiliated him in Berlin.

Hitler, Weygand was convinced, meant to trap Pétain by getting him away from Vichy and the unoccupied zone. He begged him not to go. He reminded him that Laval was incessantly in Paris, lunching with the German masters: he would betray the Marshal without turning a hair. A plot was afoot. Hitler would take revenge for his failure at Hendaye and Montoire. He would treat Pétain in Paris as he had treated Hacha of Czechoslovakia in Berlin. The Head of the State must stay in the unoccupied zone.

Late that afternoon General Laure told Laval that there would be a Council of Ministers at eight in the evening, and Laval assumed that Pétain had called the Council to announce his immediate departure for Paris. But at the appointed hour the Marshal walked into the Council Room, looking pale and nervous. 'I wish', he said, 'each Minister to sign and hand in his resignation.' The Ministers did as they were told, and for a few moments Pétain retired. When he returned he said: 'The resignations of M. Laval and M. Pipert are the only ones accepted.'

The kingmaker was ignominiously dismissed. He could hardly believe his senses and he kept asking the Marshal questions. For a time Pétain gave no direct answer. Then he said: 'I am a soldier and I like things in writing. You have never given me a report.' He wanted no trojan horsemen in his Council: and Laval, while preparing to catch the midnight train to Paris, found himself a prisoner in his former office. He was put under house arrest, and Admiral Darlan set off for the ceremony at the Invalides as the Marshal's deputy.

Three days later Laval entered the Marshal's room a freed man. In Darlan's presence Pétain offered him the Ministry of the Interior, and Laval refused. Before the day ended Pétain offered the choice between the Ministry of Agriculture and the Ministry of Industrial Production. Laval again refused. He kept his contact with Abetz, but the indignity of arrest he refused to condone. In vain Pétain insisted that the arrest had been made without his personal knowledge.

If Laval happened to be the Nazis' creature he had not yet made himself indispensable to them. They could afford to wait. The legend of Montoire was working well in Paris, and Hitler believed that he could now safely turn his attention from the West to the East. Five days after Laval's dismissal he signed the order known as 'Operation Barbarossa'. There would be war in Russia. The seizure of Gibraltar and the bases in North Africa must wait until he had smashed the Red Army with his lightning thrusts.

CHAPTER EIGHT

'I GIVE MY GLORY'

THE friend whom Lord Halifax trusted could not be ignored, and on the day after he had dismissed Laval, the Marshal sent for Professor Chevalier to make him Minister of Education. Almost at once the new Minister's powers of resistance were put to the test, for the Germans asked him to hand over some twelve hundred students and teachers from Alsace and Lorraine. Chevalier refused, and Pétain commended him. 'I am caught between two policies,' the Marshal told him later. 'One is that of collaboration with the English, which I greatly prefer. The other is the law of the conqueror, to which I am forced to submit because the conqueror is here, and he imposes it on the people whom I wish to protect against him.

'I don't practise a policy of double dealing,' he went on. 'I gave only a word. I stick to it. I am loyal with one side as with the other. With one side I signed the armistice. I respect the armistice, and that, indeed, is the desire of the English, who say that a rupture of the armistice would bring the intervention of Germany in its train. On the other hand, I am loyal and friendly with the English because within the limited scope which is allowed me— it is not very large—I do all in my power to ease their task and to get ready for their victory, which will be ours. At the same time I resist as far as I can possibly do so the German demands.' Chevalier replied that Winston Churchill knew what Pétain was doing and that he called it 'passive resistance'.

Meanwhile, flying from one desert garrison to another, General Weygand found the soldiers in North Africa dispirited by the defeat in the motherland. They had been well-trained and eager,

and, like the officers and men of the Fleet, they resented the end
to a war in which they fired not a single shot. With a candour
dangerous for German ears General Weygand urged them to prepare for the day when the military decision of 1940 would be
reversed; and he arranged for the levying of many more native
troops.

Soldiers and civilians alike were warned that the enemy wanted
to occupy the coast of North Africa and that this act, as an infringe-
ment of the armistice, must be resisted. In Marseilles German and
Italian control offices kept watch to prevent soldiers from returning to North Africa, and they made a number of arrests. Yet, in
the greatest secrecy, naval arsenals produced machine guns and
anti-tank guns for use on the other side of the Mediterranean. If
General Weygand had once held the view—so prevalent throughout France in July 1940—that Britain must soon follow her old
partner's example and accept Germany's military triumph, he read
aright the lessons of the great air battle two months later. Britain
was not giving way.

Soon the general made an indirect approach to Roosevelt for
supplies of food and petrol, and the President replied by sending
Robert Murphy to Algiers on an outwardly vague mission. The
agreement, which the visitor quickly reached with Weygand,
empowered eleven American consuls to inspect ships in the ports
of Algeria and Morocco. Roosevelt took care never to advertise
the Murphy-Weygand agreement nor to call it an agreement
between two Governments; but no one in authority in the ports
of French North Africa imagined that eleven American consuls
confined their attention to the control of food cargoes. Roosevelt,
like Weygand, was looking well ahead. He, too, understood
Pétain's 'passive resistance'. One day it would yield results.

Yet the war of passive attrition was sullied by more than one
tragic defeat. Winston Churchill was ready to accept Pétain's
word that his Government would leave alone any French colony
fighting on the side of the British. He had made a similar agreement with General de Gaulle in London that 'in no case will the

Free French forces be mobilized against the French'; but, while
Germany silently intensified her plans for the attack on Russia,
the scene within France and her territories overseas became more
baffling. In April, 1941, Admiral Darlan answered an urgent
summons to Paris, where he heard Otto Abetz demanding that
German aircraft should have the right to land at Palmyra. This
right, Abetz maintained, was like the international right of ships
of war to remain within a neutral port for twenty-four hours.
Darlan, knowing that a blunt refusal would lead to immediate
trouble, conceded the demand and hoped to play for time. Within
a week three German aircraft tried to land at Rayak, and they were
chased away. The French told the pilots that Palmyra alone had
been authorized for their use in Syria.

Difficulties were swiftly coming to a head in the Middle East,
for on May 3 Raschid Ali launched an anti-British revolt in Iraq.
In Jerusalem General Catroux, a follower of de Gaulle, clamoured
for the right to invade Syria with his troops. The lack of any
response from the British dismayed him; for although Field Marshal Wavell admitted that the Germans might use Syria and Iraq
as stepping-stones in an eastward thrust, he refused to believe that
they could make their footing in Syria easy. He meant, first of all,
to put down Raschid Ali's revolt. General Catroux then made a
grave decision; the Free French must advance on Damascus alone.
As it happened, there were no Germans in Syria, and when the
revolt in Iraq came to an ignominous end, German aircraft no
longer landed at Palmyra. The Churchill-de Gaulle accord, however, was violated. At last, after twenty months of war, Frenchman was fighting against Frenchman. To defeat was added the
bitterness of fratricide.

Amid these anxieties Darlan answered a new summons; and it
was to Berchtesgaden, where Hitler sharply renewed his old
demands upon North Africa. After insisting upon the right to use
Bizerta and Dakar, as well as the railway line between Dakar and
Gabes, the Fuehrer ordered Darlan to go straight back to Paris
and to work out the details of an agreement with Abetz. From this

'Diktat' there was no escape, save for another skilful playing for time. As far as possible, Darlan kept Pétain informed of all the negotiations, and the troubled Marshal asked Weygand to leave North Africa at once for Vichy. Weygand gave incisive advice. At this stage, he told the Council of Ministers, France ought not to make the slightest concession to Germany; it would be a betrayal of England and 'the suicide of North Africa'. Pétain agreed with him, and while Abetz was proudly boasting that he had negotiated the Protocol of Paris, the Marshal took care that the Protocol should not be ratified. In their anger the Germans called him 'Marschall Nein'.

For the moment they lacked the power to tear up the armistice, for they had turned their strength eastwards, and the lightning attack on Russia was about to begin. The circles of war were widening. France, after all, had lost only a battle; but the amazing change in the scope and scale of the war was itself a challenge to the legitimacy of Pétain's rule. Hitherto, governing France on the father-principle, he had received implicit obedience. He had required all civil servants to swear an oath of personal fidelity to him as Head of the State, and whatever their private views might have been, they steadied the ship of state. They struggled to keep the country's finances in good order, despite the burden of the Occupation costs, and the ninety cumbrous Departments of the Third Republic gave way before a healthy revival of the old provinces. Pétain set up a Council of State which had men of letters and industrialists as well as former Senators and deputies among its two hundred members; and sometimes he sought freedom from daily duties by working on a new constitution, which he made a variant of the Corporative State. He wanted to bring France more into political harmony with her Latin neighbours.

Numbed by the swiftness of defeat, his countrymen would have accepted Pétain's constitution, if it had been ready, in the autumn of 1940, or even in the spring of 1941; but French intelligence played unceasingly within the darkness. It took into account both Pétain's shortcomings and his inhuman difficulties. The silence which fell upon France had been in part unreal, for many thousands of her workers followed the Communist directions. Molotov's pact with Ribbentrop on the eve of the war had suddenly confronted them with a clash of loyalties. The hurt to instinctive patriotism was deep; but, as Communists, these workers made no attempt to resist the German onrush.

The mask was now off. Stalin's war against Hitler was the workers' war. Communists became a spearhead of the gathering resistance within France. They drew sympathy from many who were not Marxists. The thoughtful were not content with a negative attitude. They recognized discipline, the spirit of sacrifice, the impatience to remove social injustices. Only a few middle-class standards were left for them to maintain; the food-queue and the fireless living-room were social levellers. Believers were no longer anxious to identify the Church with established order. When freedom was restored, they would live and work as Catholic Democrats.

Among the men passing judgment on the Government's actions was the disgraced Pierre Laval. He kept away from Vichy to divide his time between Paris and his country home at Chateldon. He knew well how to dissimulate, and he realized that the public words of Pétain or Darlan bore no relation to their thoughts or their plans. Yet he was shocked to find how little the men around the Marshal cared to keep their ears to the ground and to listen to the voices which were muted through fear of the secret police. He saw in the aged hero many strains of obstinacy and fanaticism, and he was soon convinced that Pétain lacked political assurance. A true weapon of freedom in France is ridicule, and Laval guessed that people were laughing when a Vichy scribe extolled 'a benevolent Marshal, supremely wise, good and far-seeing', who exercised his authority through 'provincial intendants, protectors of local custom and of local dialects, folksongs and folklore'.

The language which fear of the secret police made people whisper had nothing to do with folksongs and folklore. Here was the political language which Englishmen and Americans could speak openly; and it was the language which, from his head-quarters in London, Charles de Gaulle could not ignore. At heart the leader of the Free French was authoritarian. He had steeped himself in Cartesian philosophy; he stood aloof from the mundane soldiery and assumed that destiny chose him for an exalted task. He brought to London not a little of the traditional French distrust of 'perfidious Albion', and for a time he feared that the British desired to seize North Africa for themselves. He was not prepared to see Fighting France—the France which refused to accept the armistice—limited to the battlefield. Pétain was the pretending France, and he was the real France. 'You had the merit,' he was to tell Winston Churchill, 'after the armistice, to back the French card. This card is called de Gaulle; do not lose it now.' Yet it was impossible for him to escape from the political climate of war-time London, and his advisers let him know what were the hopes and dreams of his followers. They were fighting for a people's rule. They would never put on the garments of a Corporative State already turned to shabbiness. The Fourth Republic would be the Third Republic dry-cleaned.

Three months went by, and the lightning war on Russia had not been brought to a brilliant conclusion. The earth was scorched but the spirit of resistance in the East remained unyielding. Comforting paternal words from Vichy began to sound like a dead language; and when at last the Government produced, in October, a Charter of Labour, people scorned its Corporative manner. So elaborate were its clauses, the *Temps* complained, it remained 'as hermetically sealed to any worker who set out to read it as a poem by Mallarmé'. The mood of the people was becoming militant. Everywhere a hidden resistance stretched its tentacles, and the Germans let their anger get the upper hand. Before October was out, they shot fifty men whom they were holding as hostages at Chateaubriant. Among them was the seventeen-year-old son of a Communist deputy.

At seven the next morning Pétain summoned a member of his staff. 'You have read the news, du Moulin? They have shot fifty hostages. We cannot stay here any longer. We are dishonoured. All this bloodshed recoils on us.'

M. du Moulin de la Barthete scarcely knew how to reply. He saw a man whose eyes were filled with tears, whose voice seemed far away, who had suddenly become a hundred years old. 'We must protest, Monsieur le Maréchal,' he said.

'Oh! Protest, protest. Yes, we will go and protest. But that's not enough. We must throw ourselves in their way. We must stop this killing.'

'What can we do?'

'I have thought hard about it. I have not shut an eye all night. I must go to Paris and make myself a prisoner.'

'You, Monsieur le Maréchal?'

'Yes, I. I wish to be the only hostage.'

Pétain meant what he said, and one or two devoted followers declared that they would follow his example. Like the Marshal, they packed their bags. After luncheon Pétain called his Ministers for a farewell meeting. Right through the afternoon they pleaded with him, His act, they said, would grieve the people and leave them leaderless. A German Gauleiter would take his place. No one would remain to stand firmly by the armistice or to work, though with only a partial success, for the return of the prisoners, the stricken manhood of France.

The old man stayed at his post. He went on bargaining in a stubborn way with Nazi masters, and though they soon intensified their demands for labour in Germany, he would not allow one woman worker to go to the land of the foe. He had given the order for de Gaulle to be tried in his absence and he endorsed the condemnation to death; but he also made sure that the dependants of the Fighting French received their allowances. He was often tired and sometimes dispirited. He did not doubt that the Germans resented his refusal to ratify the Protocol of Paris, and in November—when they knew that war was about to break over the Pacific —they compelled him to withdraw Weygand from North Africa.

As soon as Weygand had retired to Cannes, Goering arranged

to meet Pétain at Saint-Florentin on December 1. A man denied his best adviser on North Africa might have been an easy prey, but Pétain, now 85, braced all his nerves for the ordeal. The powerful Goering must see again the splendid figure which he had known at a King's funeral in Belgrade. The German began the talk in a conciliatory manner. The time had come, he said, for a stronger defence in North Africa, and it might be necessary to re-mobilize the Air Force and the Navy.

Pétain interrupted him with a ready answer. He agreed to arrange the re-mobilization, but only if 'you give us back our officers, our non-commissioned officers, our men and the material with which to re-make our formations'. Collaboration, he went on, was possible only when promises were kept. 'I have understood', he said, 'that collaboration meant treating as between one equal and another. If the conqueror is on top and the conquered underfoot, there is no more collaboration. It is what you call a "Diktat" and what we call "the law of the stongest". In 1919 France committed the error of not making a peace of collaboration. She won the war; she lost the peace. You can win the war alone; you cannot make the peace alone. You cannot make peace without France. By not making a peace of collaboration you are liable to lose the peace. Think over what I have said to you.'

This bluntness astonished Goering. 'Tell me,' he hectored, 'who are the victors? Are we, or are you?'

Never before, Pétain replied, had he been more conscious of France's defeat; but 'I am confident of France's future and her revival. As for me personally, you must know that it is easy for a man of my age to make the transition from life to death.'

Within a week he completed a memornadum for Hitler, in which he discussed all the issues which Goering had mentioned. Were the Germans, he asked, dissatisfied with France's agricultural output? They should release the eight hundred thousand landworkers who were still their prisoners. Were they complaining about the faulty distribution of goods? They should return the railway trucks which had not yet come back from Germany.

'French industry is not producing enough. You should supply it
with coal and other primary materials. We are waiting for them';
and Pétain dared to tell Hitler that he had designed the demarca-
tion-line 'as a bleeding wound in the bowels of France'. He went
on to protest against the heavy costs of the occupation. If they
were once needed for the maintenance of a million men, the
German Army in France now numbered only half a million:
'already the sum paid to the account of the costs of the Army
occupation, before there has been any discussion and settlement of
the war indemnity, greatly exceeds the total sum which Germany
paid after her defeat in 1918'.

Though the memorandum was bold, Pétain did not attempt to
tear down the appearances of collaboration with the Germans and
coldness towards the British. Triumphs went unrecorded. Hurts
which he could not avoid earned him the contempt of the people
whom he served. He was at war, and the first casualty in war is
truth. He knew now that the people were restive and that many
would condemn the league of French volunteers which had been
formed to fight against the Russians on an eastern front. These
men put on German uniforms and were to share the fortunes of
war with a Blue Division which Franco sent from Spain. Their
numbers were negligible, but Pétain agreed to be the league's
patron. He was deceiving the enemy. He was creating bonds with
Franco and making it more difficult for Hitler to demand access to
Gibraltar through Spain.

As 1941—the year of the invasion of Russia and the attack on
Pearl Harbour—drew to its close, Pétain turned again to the task
of writing a constitution. He was still in no hurry to complete
it, for now, despite the swift engulfing of Indo-China by the
Japanese, he could think about the day when the last German
soldier should leave France. 'The constitution is a long-term job,'
he told General Hering. 'I cannot think of promulgating a constitution so long as the Germans are in France. Besides, I am not
charged with the duty of promulgating a new constitution, but
with preparing it.' The writing of a constitution allowed a brief

escape from the shows and fantasies of collaboration. Yet there
was no way of speaking frankly to the people. The moves of
diplomatic attrition could be known only to the players. Silence
wore a treasonable look.

The fear that this look was deceptive haunted the foe. In Paris
Laval sensed the worsening of French relations with the Germans.
More repressive measures, he believed, were about to be imposed,
and Vichy, still outwardly a spa for ageing invalids, had little
awareness of the German mood. Laval, therefore, sought and
obtained an interview with Goering, whom he found seated in his
own former study in the Quai d'Orsay. If he meant to convince
Goering that good will might lead to a lasting peace between Germany and France, he was disappointed. Goering was far from
conciliatory, and he spoke bitter words of his interview with
Pétain at Saint-Florentin. 'We have seen the light,' he said, in
substance, 'and we know that we were mistaken. Henceforth we
shall treat France with the same hostility that she has shown so
clearly towards us.'

As soon as Pétain heard that Laval had spoken with Goering,
he arranged to meet his former Minister in the forest at Randan.
What he heard distressed him: the 'two-face' policy, as Laval
called it, was certainly not succeeding. He begged Laval to see
Admiral Darlan and to give him a fuller report of the interview;
and when Darlan went to Chateldon he brought from the Marshal
an invitation to re-enter the Government. Laval did not give an
immediate reply.

Meanwhile the Germans were faced with a new annoyance, and
it came from the crowded courtroom at Riom. In the early days of
the Vichy regime several prominent leaders of the Third Republic
were put under arrest, and now—on February 19, 1942—Edouard
Daladier, Léon Blum and General Gamelin were brought to their
trial. The long postponement had been a searing scandal and the
prisoners defended themselves with eloquence and skill. They
became again the spokesmen of France; the men of the resistance
answering the men of the armistice. They were charged with fail-

ure to prepare France for war. Above all, they were charged
explicitly for their negligence from March, 1936, when Hitler sent
troops to the Rhineland, to the outbreak of the war; and the
charge angered Hitler. He wanted the prisoners to be tainted with
war guilt, not with appeasement.

In the days of peace the forum for the statesmen had been the
Chamber of Deputies. Now it was the dock, from which their
words took wing over the conquered land. 'Gentlemen,' said
Blum, 'I have finished. You are free to condemn us, but I do not
think that you will be able to efface our work. I do not think,
though this may, perhaps, appear arrogant, that you will be able
to remove us from the pages of our history. In this belief there is
something of pride, but nothing of presumption. At a time of
great national danger, we personified, we gave new life to democracy and republicanism, which are the true traditions of our
country. We shall have been, at least, one moment in the history
of those traditions. We do not represent some monstrous excres-
cence in our national history, for our Government was of the
people. We were continuing what has been our national way of
life since the French Revolution. We did not sever the links of
that chain. We forged another link; we tightened the chain . . . By
a cruel irony, gentlemen, this fidelity is now held to be treason.
Yet fidelity is not exhausted. It still lives, and France will one day
reap its fruits.'

The dock was too dangerous both for paternalism and for the
façade of collaboration, and when the Riom trial had lasted for
seven weeks the authorities in Vichy suddenly ordered its adjourn-
ment; and it was never re-opened. The war which had brought
France to defeat had now changed its character, and the cruelty of
German rule would become more naked. Goering voiced the Nazi
verdict that France was a proved deceiver; and when Laval went
back to Vichy to rejoin the Council of Ministers Sauckel arrived
in Paris to tighten the Gestapo machinery. Brutal orders would
circulate even through the unoccupied zone. Laval, like Pétain
and Darlan, must constantly dissimulate and play for time.

Was he patriot or collaborator? Pétain never found the key to a baffling personality, whose rude charm left no one alone, not even Otto Abetz. In his presence the Marshal felt distrust and discomfort, and yet he still believed that at heart the man was a patriot. Laval was clever, intuitive and ingenious; and he barely concealed his contempt for Pétain's political judgments. If he was the most hated man in France, he gloried in his unpopularity. On one fateful occasion General Weygand told him bluntly that ninety-five per cent of the people of France opposed his policy. 'You are joking, my dear general,' Laval replied. 'It's not ninety-five per cent of the people who oppose my policy. It's ninety-eight per cent. But I know what is good for them.'

No Vichy scribe could adequately explain why this unpopular Minister, whom the Marshal once dismissed and arrested, had come back to office. He was back, people felt sure, on his own terms. The hero of Verdun began to appear like a man of straw. Though nature had given him wisdom, there comes a time when ripeness turns to decay. When Pétain made his peace with Laval, he was already 86; and 'the life of this old majesty', perhaps, was far exceeding the span of years which Shakespeare envisaged for King Lear.

There was ebbing strength, but no lack of watchfulness. Neither to the Marshal in Saint-Florentin nor to Laval in Paris had Goering mentioned Poland, but so long as there was a German soldier left in France Pétain could not rid himself of the fear that the motherland might become a second Poland. This was the spectre which gave so sharp an edge to the conqueror's threats. North Africa, too, stood in danger of attack, and when the Germans compelled him to recall General Weygand, the Marshal chose General Juin to take his place.

General Juin had been a prisoner-of-war, and Pétain asked for his release. The Germans gave him his freedom on condition that he never took up arms against them, and they were pleased by his appointment to North Africa. He was well practised in dissimulation with the enemy, but his ties with Pétain were not intimate.

L

Far closer to Pétain was Darlan, who understood exactly the diplomatic attrition and who was prepared, if the Marshal lost his freedom, to act independently in North Africa. Some secret advice —as unknown, perhaps, to Pétain in Vichy as to de Gaulle in London—may have made him prolong a stay in Algiers.

On the night of November 7, 1942, Robert Murphy called on General Juin and said: 'American forces are landing tonight in North Africa. They come not as enemies, but as friends of France.' For a moment Juin was silent. Then he said: 'Admiral Darlan is my superior, the representative of Marshal Pétain.'

Only a few hours beforehand Germans in La Linea and Algeciras had seen a vast concourse of ships passing Gibraltar. They believed that the convoy was steaming for Malta, and at once the Axis aircraft were made ready to deliver a knock-out blow. But the convoy, after heading for Malta, turned about, and the landings in North Africa took the Germans by surprise. General Eisenhower, who was in command, did not know what resistance he was likely to meet. At the moment, however, the French had no choice save to resist. Even when their officers realized the weight of the assault, they remembered their oaths to the Marshal; they must resist until the right words came from Vichy.

Pétain, taken unawares, was deeply perplexed. The fighting had raged for about twelve hours when a message reached Laval from Hitler. It told him that a mere rupture of diplomatic relations with the Anglo-Saxon Powers would not be enough. 'France will have to declare war on the English and the Americans. If the French Government is prepared to adopt a clear-cut policy Germany is prepared to march side by side with France through thick and thin.' Laval and the Marshal, however, rejected Hitler's offer without even consulting the Council of Ministers.

In the confusion of battle Darlan received a German demand to land aircraft. He wired to Vichy but instructions did not reach him until the 9th. By that time Laval was on his way to Munich with Abetz. He had been summoned by Hitler, and he guessed aright that the encounter would be stormy. For two hours he was kept waiting outside Hitler's door only to be told that the Germans would chase the intruders out of North Africa. 'You must know', Hitler declared, 'that France, from this day forth, will be permitted to keep only those portions of her Empire which she is able to defend.'

Laval's summons to Munich, however, did not deprive Pétain of an adviser, for Weygand slipped quietly out of Cannes to be near him. The two soldiers were together when, on the 10th, the American armistice terms reached Vichy from Darlan. Both agreed that they must be accepted, and a telephone call was put through to Munich. Laval, not yet recovered from his audience with the Fuehrer, spoke excitedly. If the terms were accepted, he said, he would have to leave France because the reprisals would be terrible.

Open telegrams and open telephone calls were alike snares; and after he had listened to Laval, Pétain sent a second telegram to Darlan stating: ' I ordered you to defend North Africa. I stick to that order.' At first Darlan read the message as a betrayal, and he surrendered to the Americans. Almost at once, however, he got a secret message: 'Understand that the order was necessary for negotiations in course.' Ostensibly the Marshal chose General Nogues to take Darlan's place as his representative in North Africa; but a second secret telegram to Darlan explained: 'It is solely because you are supposed prisoner that you have not been nominated representative of the Marshal in Africa.'

General Nogues told Darlan to go ahead with the armistice talks, and meanwhile he asked Pétain for an open approval of what he and Darlan were doing; for they had to convince the officers and men that the Marshal was behind them. Pétain's staff, as a matter of duty, told Laval, who had returned from Munich. At first Laval seemed to approve; but he was soon on the telephone to Abetz. A third secret message was sent to Darlan: 'Intimate understanding between Marshal and President but, before replying, occupation authorities are being consulted.' Darlan, when he got this message, saw only one interpretation; the Mar-

shal himself approved. He had obeyed Pétain. Nothing else mattered; and without further delay he released all officers from their
oath of allegiance to the Head of the State. On the 12th, the
armistice was signed, and the resistance which had cost eleven
thousand French lives was soon turned into a Franco-American
partnership.

Laval was right when he said that the reprisals would be terrible.
The Germans ended the armistice abruptly. Their soldiers tore
down the demarcation posts and swept across the once unoccupied
zone. They disbanded the little army which the armistice had
allowed to France and they took away its arms. On November 17
they ordered Pétain and Laval to arrange for a declaration of war
on the United States within twenty-four hours, and they told
Pétain to denounce the African desertions. Neither Pétain nor
Laval obeyed. Then came the orders to seize the Fleet in Toulon.

Naval commanders knew what they had to do. They obeyed
Darlan's secret order and scuttled the ships. Officers and men
stood strictly to attention while the German military police per-
formed the ritual of their arrest. That a word might be honoured
and kept unsullied France gave her Fleet to the absolving
waters.

Some who had a ready access to the Marshal begged him at
once to leave Vichy for North Africa. He alone could raise aloft
the standard of fighting France and so end the cleavage between
Pétainist and Gaullist. On African soil all parties could sink their
differences and forget the unhappy past. An aeroplane was at hand
to take Pétain away. He refused to go. He would never leave
France of his own accord until she was free. His place was with the
people in 1940, and it was with them now.

For a long time his authority had dwindled. Now it was suddenly cut off. Henceforward there was no armistice with Germany
to use as a shield and buckler. The Gestapo, the racial laws, the
forced labour, the communal punishments and the shooting of
hostages would ravage France to the painful eve of her liberation.
Since the people would know little escape from suffering, Pétain

must share it with them. He would stand condemned for deeds he
dared not explain. In June, 1940, he had said: 'I make France the
gift of my person.' Now he said: 'I give my glory.'

To those around him Pétain kept on saying: 'A pilot should
stay at the tiller in a storm.' That, as André François-Poncet
remarked more than twelve years later, was his greatest error; 'for
the tiller slipped away from him'. For one thing, he was deprived
of the two men whose judgment and advice he valued. General
Weygand, expecting arrest, decided to avoid Cannes and to find a
quiet lodging in the countryside. Laval induced him, first of all,
to make a call at Chateldon and, as he drove away, he found a car,
filled with SS men, running alongside his own, which was pushed
into a ditch. He was arrested, and he spent the next twenty-four
hours in a journey to a German fortress.

Darlan, too, was beyond the Marshal's reach. Though the
Americans disliked the authoritarian manner of his brief rule in
North Africa, they did not interfere. For some, indeed, the
Admiral was not authoritarian enough. Among them was Bonnier
de la Chapelle, the twenty-years-old son of a quiet schoolmaster.
He nursed dreams of a restored monarchy, and his hero was the
Comte de Paris. More than once he sought an interview with
Darlan, and on Christmas Eve his wish was granted. His appoint-
ment gave him the right of entry to the vestibule of the main
Government building, and when he saw the Admiral approaching
his office, he shot him dead. In his cell the impenitent youth vainly
awaited liberation by the royalists. He was allowed no trial, and
early on Boxing Day he faced the firing squad.

The more the war lengthened, the more archaic seemed the
creed of Darlan's fanatical assailant. American Democracy and
Russian Communism were twisted into twin facets of political
freedom. Both in the East and in the West the war was being waged
for the liberation of the common man. Hierarchy, privilege, the
rule of the many by the few belonged to the era which resistance
to Hitler had suddenly uprooted. Men wanted to unfurl their sails,
not to trim them. They were impatient with the past, and for that

reason they made a hero of Charles de Gaulle, who had foreseen the nature of the fighting and shown his bewildered countrymen how a successful tank battle could be fought. His words on the radio were eloquent and compelling. He moved from London to Algiers, and he soon proved himself to be a stronger man than General Giraud, who had succeeded Darlan. He became the true leader in the eyes of nearly all resisters, and he had the daring to declare a moral war in which Catholics and Communists alike could take part. His language was both traditional and modern.

Outwardly France was placid. Men and women went about their work as though they were not unduly troubled. The theatre in Paris was brilliant. Elegant nursemaids pushed perambulators past the stately gates of 84 Avenue Foch, not realizing that the cellars of the mansion had become the Gestapo's torture-chambers. Yet imperceptibly the numbers of the resisters rose. The Fresnes prison was filled with patriots, and when the army was disbanded many soldiers quietly embraced the discipline of resistance.

The more the Germans tightened the screws and intensified their demands, the more threadbare wore the pretences of collaboration. Allied aircraft bombed railway stations and marshalling yards, and casualties were heavy among railwaymen. They did not complain, for they were zealous resisters. Many listened while the London radio told them of the exploits of French soldiers fighting under General Juin in North Africa and, later, in Italy; and when the enemy was driven out of Corsica they re-furbished their pride in the Napoleonic legend. The hour of liberation was drawing nearer.

Resistance took innumerable forms. Intelligence played against stupidity, miscalculation and psychological clumsiness, for the foe was often far from clever. Eminent writers—among them Julien Benda, François Mauriac and Jacques Maritain—wrote for the *Editions de Minuit*, which passed surreptitiously from one household to another. For this series Jean Bruller wrote *Silence de la Mer*, in which he described the response of a sensitive Nazi to the discovery of French civilization; and it was typical of the movement that Bruller should have used a pen-name, Vercors. Resistance was for France, not for personal recognition or prestige.

The Head of the State still inspected the veterans of another war. He saw aged and bemedalled men exulting in pride as he asked them in which battle on the Western front they had earned their decorations. Those who were left had grown old, and their memories were long, like a green tooth. It was often the very young, impatient with the hoary legend of Verdun, who risked their lives helping a British or American airman to get out of France.

Pétain himself knew the strength of the resistance. He frequently received Prince François-Xavier de Bourbon, a claimant to the Spanish throne, who sought his help in setting condemned men free. Once the prince asked him whether it was true that he had seen the Prince Napoleon or one of the princes of Orleans, and Petain replied: 'My door is open to all Frenchmen, whether princes or workers or peasants. My door is open to everyone. Mark this and remember: I am neither Imperialist nor Royalist. I try to save what can be saved of the French State from this catastrophe. After me, and at the peace, we must inevitably go back to the Republic.' On another occasion he told the prince of his own plight. 'You know that I am a prisoner,' he said. 'I cannot write a letter which might not be censored. I cannot use the telephone without being heard. I cannot make a speech which is not submitted beforehand.'

Yet he was not completely powerless. By a look or a gesture he showed whom he wished to praise or whom to admonish. Nor did he forget that his authority as Head of the State was vested in him by the National Assembly. Though the Senate and the Chamber of Deputies were prorogued, they could not be abolished before the nation had ratified a new constitution. The power to rule by decree came to the Head of the State from the National Assembly. Pétain decided, therefore, to make sure that no man, not even Laval, should claim to be his successor before obtaining the deliberate sanction of the National Assembly. Thus—on November 12, 1943—'We, Marshal of France, Head of the French State, decreed that, in the event of "our" demise before the nation had ratified the new constitution, the constituent power must go back to the Senate and the Chamber. All agreements made since July 10, 1940, which would limit the play and exercise of the rights of the National Assembly "are and remain repealed".'

This was his last card, and it failed him. A sharp letter from the German Ministry of Foreign Affairs announced that he must submit the text of all laws and decrees to the Government of the Reich. Moreover, he must allow Laval to reform the French Government and to make it more acceptable to the Germans. Pétain realized that he was beaten. Laval was France's ruler now, but he ruled by German sufferance. The façade of friendship between victor and vanquished was smashed.

But now the victor's status was put in peril, for a new battle of France was soon to begin. German divisions moved westwards again, and the whole country fell under a full military occupation. At last the long patience, which Pétain often preached, would be rewarded. Once he had scorned the handful of divisions which the British were sending back to France after Dunkirk and he had refused to place any faith in Reynaud's appeals to Roosevelt. But Churchill kept his word; he was helping to bring liberation to France. The process, as the 'machine-minder' general of other years knew only too well, had demanded exhaustive preparation and precise planning. Armour must drive out armour. The enemy must know no rest from the overpowering assaults of aeroplanes and tanks.

Pétain awaited, and yet dreaded, this new battle. Would the homeless crowd the roads again? Loyalties, Pétainist or Gaullist, would not save them from the fury of a foe put violently on the defensive. Whether the process ended in liberation or in a perpetual enslavement, the people would be tortured with doubt and pain; except as a prisoner, the Marshal would never leave them. He meant to stay in Vichy and to await the arrival of old comrades-in-arms. They might judge and condemn him, but he would be faithful to the end.

Within the first week of August, 1944, the Allies had pushed the Germans out of Normandy, and Laval, realizing that their tanks might soon rattle down the Champs-Élysées, went to Paris to fulfil two self-chosen missions; to urge the Germans not to defend the capital, and to summon the National Assembly. Now that the people had no more use for the Marshal's rule by decree he would call the Republic back to life. He even persuaded Otto Abetz to let him go to Nancy and to bring back Edouard Herriot as a free man, so that he might preside once more over the Chamber of Deputies. He was acting too late, for stern orders soon reached Abetz from Berlin; the members of the French Government were to go to Belfort. In vain Laval declared that he was not leaving Paris, for Abetz replied that he was ready to use force. Laval called the Ministers together. They knew that the Vichy Cabinet was meeting for the last time, and on the morning of August 17 Gestapo cars drew up outside the Hotel Matignon to take them away.

As soon as Pétain heard that Laval had left Paris under restraint, he knew that his own turn was imminent. He, therefore, summoned the Papel Nuncio and the Swiss Minister to his apartment. They were on their way when two Germans, de Renthe-Finck and General von Neubronn, demanded an audience. Laval and other members of the French Government, de Renthe-Finck told Pétain, had already left Paris for Belfort of their own free will. This was too much for Admiral Blehaut, who was in the room. 'It is a tissue of lies,' he cried. 'We know perfectly well that M. Laval has been taken away by force.'

'Admiral, you have no right to speak to me in this way.'

'I have the right. I am a military man, not a diplomat. I speak of things as they are.'

For his own safety, de Renthe-Finck declared, the Marshal should leave, and he began to read a list of the men who were to go with him. As soon as Admiral Blehaut heard his own name, he blurted out: 'I am not under the orders of the Germans. I am under the orders of the Marshal. The Marshal does not want to go. The matter is settled.'

General von Neubronn intervened. 'Admiral,' he said, 'if you don't want to leave, I have the means of making you do so.'

A note was passed to Admiral Bléhaut telling him that the Papal Nuncio and the Swiss Minister were now in the next room. He asked that they should enter.

The two Ministers walked into the room, and the Germans betrayed their surprise. In his anger de Renthe-Finck said to General von Neubronn: 'This is infamy. This is a matter between Frenchmen and Germans, and not one to be discussed before foreign Ministers. It is absolutely essential for us to leave.'

None the less, the Nuncio and the Swiss Minister saw them leaving. 'See, Monseigneur,' the Admiral cried. 'See, Monsieur le Ministre. These gentlemen dare not repeat before you the unpardonable ultimatum which they addressed to the Marshal.'

Later General von Neubronn came back with a number of SS men. They entered the Marshal's room, and they took their prisoners away.

Pétain was removed from Belfort to Morvillars, and from Morvillars to Sigmaringen. Though a French Commission was set up on German soil, he would have nothing to do with it; for he was the Germans' prisoner. His one desire, as the war drew towards its close, was to get back to France, and he was dismayed to hear that de Gaulle had ordered a trial for treason. The charge of treason, he insisted, was unjust; and to be tried contumaciously was the last degradation. Since he must defend his honour, it was imperative to reach France before the legal process against him was due to begin. The Germans, however, had no intention of handing him over, and on the night of April 21 they removed him from Sigmaringen to the castle of Zell in Wurtemburg. The old man imagined that the Germans were carrying him to their half-mythical central redoubt, and he declared that, except to go back to France, he would not leave Zell.

Even Zell was no longer safe from the Allied advance. The sweep of events confused the Germans who were guarding Pétain, and when they lost all contact with Ribbentrop they offered to conduct their prisoner to the Swiss frontier. Pétain replied that he would leave for the frontier when the Swiss Government signed a guarantee and allowed a Swiss diplomat to join the convoy. Many hours passed, but through the night of April 23 Pétain drove towards Switzerland. Allied bombing was incessant, and even the car in which he travelled seemed to have been made a target. At nine, on the morning of April 24, he reached the frontier.

On the same day—so great was his haste—he entered France. The prisoner of the Germans was now the prisoner of his own countrymen. It was his 89th birthday.

CHAPTER NINE

CONDEMNED

GENERAL DE GAULLE had not wanted to give the order that Marshal Pétain should be tried contumaciously. Secretly, it was said, he hoped that the Swiss Government would refuse the French demand for his extradition. It was the Marshal himself who had forced the issue, and he was lodged in a small and bare room in the hideous fort of Montrouge. In the adjoining room was his wife, who, as the chief hostess in Vichy, had 'intelligence with the enemy'.

Trial was inevitable. Five tormenting yeears had turned veneration and trust into hatred and contempt. People whom the Germans shot as hostages numbered thousands. Three-quarters of a million Frenchmen had gone to Germany for forced labour. Nearly a quarter million were punished for their politics or their race. Against these sufferers for France stood about one hundred thousand of her citizens on whom fell the stigma of collaboration with the enemy. These men of Vichy could not be brought to justice fairly if the former Head of the State were allowed his freedom.

People, however, were not waiting for the judgment of the High Court. They debated among themselves where lay the Marshal's guilt—in asking for an armistice; in making cruel concessions to the victor; in refusing to leave France when the Americans had landed in North Africa. They were not prepared to be detached. At the airport of Le Bourget military honours were given to returning prisoners-of-war as, dressed in rags, they walked across the tarmac; and many felt their blood running cold whenever they saw a lorry filled with emaciated and shaven-headed men rescued from Buchenwald or Dachau. The Marshal's trial, like Joan's, would be political and end with a political verdict. Pétain, like Joan, stood condemned by the hazards of war. Compiègne entrapped them both.

Nevertheless, the condemnation had to be strictly legal, and the prosecutors for the Government based their charges on article 87 and article 75 of the French penal code. Article 87 made it an offence to take office 'with the object of destroying or changing the form of government'; and article 75 made it an act of treason, to be punished with death, for a Frenchman to have intelligence 'with a foreign power or with its agents with the view of supporting the activities of that power against France'. Once the charges were stated Pétain had to choose his defending counsel. The task was not easy. The few barristers whom he had known well were dead. One eminent lawyer, who was approached, dared not risk the odium of sympathy with the chief of collaborators. Another, whose name was suggested to him, Pétain scornfully rejected because he had defended the witty and infamous murderer, Landru.

At last, on the advice of Madame Debeney, wife of a general who shared his German captivity at Sigmaringen, Pétain chose Fernand Payen, a man 73 years old and Dean of the Paris Bar. Payen agreed to defend him, and then he got ready for a combat with the most formidable prosecutor of the age, for his opponent was the hard and brilliant André Mornet. In the year of the mutiny Mornet was remorselessly prosecuting Mata Hari, a world-famous and lovely Dutch dancer, for espionage. Many influential men tried to save her reputation and her life; but Mornet's exposure was complete and brutal, and Mata Hari went to her death at Vincennes. Mornet was now an old man, but he had been fired with enthusiasm for the Gaullist cause. To secure the Marshal's condemnation would be to crown a notable career.

As Payen needed a junior counsel to help him, he asked for Jacques Isorni, a barrister not yet 34, who had vainly tried to

prevent the execution of Robert Brassilach, a Paris journalist.
Isorni was a Breton whose ancestress had rocked the cradle of the
King of Rome. His Celtic imagination often fed on the sadness of
Napoleon's last six years spent on a lonely island. Great men, he
was certain, were always misjudged when people neglected to
study their real motives. He was a former soldier who had kept
his admiration for Pétain; and, since there was still no bus service,
he walked exultantly to Montrouge.

Payen had chosen his assistant well. The prisoner took an
immediate delight in the company of a man more than half a century younger than himself. He became fatherly without a trace of
aloofness. He was playful, ironic and amused. though sometimes
the talk betrayed the hovering dread of death. 'What can they do
to me?' he asked.

'Condemn you to death,' Isorni said quietly.

'I know. The London radio even said that they would shoot
me with my face against the wall.'

At another meeting he referred again to the infamy of such a
position, which he seemed to fear even more than death. Consol-
ingly Payen had said: 'This can be arranged,' and in his deafness
Pétain thought that the old Dean was hinting at suicide. For a
moment his face was flushed with anger.

There was not, in fact, complete sympathy between Payen and
the prisoner. Payen was upright, but conventional. The easiest
way of securing an acquittal, he believed was to plead that the
Marshal's intellect had become enfeebled. This shocked and dismayed Pétain. He was willing enough to admit that he had made
grievous mistakes, but he was also convinced that he had fought
the enemy with the only weapons available to him. Here he had
the support of the young Isorni, who begged Payen to let him
play a more active part in his defence; and the first time he succeeded in going to Montrouge alone, he spoke frankly with Pétain
and outlined his own scheme of defence. The Marshal, he argued,
was still sovereign. His defence must be purposeful and active, like
the defence of Joan or King Louis the Sixteenth. He must be justi-

fied in the eyes of the world. Pétain agreed, and his wife, who was listening, took Isorni by the arm. 'There is a current between you,' she said.

The obstacle was Payen, bent on securing an acquittal with as little trouble as possible; but Isorni was anxious to show that the Head of the State had pursued a deliberate and intelligent policy and that he had retained his sharpness of judgment. Isorni suggested that he should be helped by a barrister who had been active in the resistance, and Pétain gave an eager approval. The helper was Jean Lamaire, whom hitherto Isorni had not known. The newcomer accepted Isorni's approach to the defence and, greatly daring, he went to Payen to tell him that the Marshal wanted his defence to be conducted in Isorni's way.

Long hours of legal interrogation stood before the aged prisoner. He received a few chosen callers, and they included General Juin. With courtesy and simplicity of bearing Pétain wore down the asperities of prison-life and brought out the natural gentleness of his custodian, M. Simon. 'We must always be near to the humble, near to the little men,' he said. 'They are the only ones that matter.'

Payen let Isorni frame the defence, but he was still reluctant to abandon the plea of enfeeblement. Where mistakes were made, he liked to see the blame attached to other men, and particularly to Laval, whom he detested; but Pétain would not consent. 'I can't do that,' he said. 'He was my Minister. Besides, I never doubted his love of France.'

Minutely Pétain prepared the statement which he was to make in the High Court. He promised that it would be his only contribution to the trial. He would ask and answer no questions. Once he had made his statement he would treat the rest of his trial with a stoical silence. The statement was his personal defence and, therefore, its meaning must be exact. 'General de Gaulle writes well,' he said, 'but he lacks simplicity.'

That was an aside uttered while he was carefully chiselling his own defence. He examined each word, and each time he made a change, the barristers admitted, the new word yielded a greater precision. 'Do you forget, gentlemen, that I belong to the French Academy?'

When Pétain and the young barristers had agreed upon the statement, it was shown to Payen, who suggested some clumsy or commonplace alterations. Isorni protested. 'We can't make changes at the last minute,' he said. 'We have thought out each phrase'; and, turning to the prisoner, he added: 'It's so much your style.' With irony Pétain replied: 'So this is the style that befits your clients? What if you were Bossuet's advocate?' And he quoted from Bossuet's funeral oration for the Prince of Condé: *Restait cette redoubtable infanterie de l'armée d'Espagne.*

Did Payen believe that he was in physical or mental decay? Then, at the trial, he would read the statement without glasses, and he made no comment when the young men wrote it out in a large hand. He decided how he would be dressed for the trial. He would wear the simplest uniform permitted to the Marshal of France. His only decoration would be the Military Medal. Isorni and Lemaire wanted him to take the Marshal's baton into the court. 'No, no,' he answered. 'It would be theatrical.'

Members of the jury were chosen on a strict principle. Twelve came from the minority of deputies who—on July 10, 1940—had voted against granting special powers to the Marshal. The other twelve came from the resistance workers. All were the prisoner's opponents, and some were Communists. The trial was bound to have its moments of passion, and about five hundred French or foreign journalists expected to be given Press tickets. Like members of the Consultative Assembly, they debated where the trial would take place—at the Chamber of Deputies, the palace of Versailles or the large central hall of the Court of Appeal?—and great was the disappointment when the Government, fearing an attempt at assassination, chose the minute Appeal Court within the Palace of Justice because it was easy to guard. Two ill-lit robing rooms were set aside to house the Marshal and his wife throughout the trial; and on Sunday, July 22, a black prison-van was driven out of Montrouge. It took the prisoner and Madame la Maréchale Pétain to the heavily guarded Palace of Justice.

Early the next morning the little courtroom was already crowded with people, and photographers stood round the chair which was to serve as the dock. The hubbub increased and the heat became almost oppressive. Then there was a sudden hush, and as the Marshal strode into the court, all rose from their seats. It was like a spontaneous act of homage, and some, recollecting their error, explained that they had stood up to get a better view of the prisoner. He was tall, self-composed, debonair. His back was straight, and the whiteness of his moustache accentuated a still youthful complexion. He had made sure that none could pity him for decrepitude and old age.

Only a few yards away sat André Mornet. He was heavily robed, and he wore above his ermine collar the chain of the Legion of Honour. The court was his theatre; but as he gazed at the soldier who was his senior by nearly fifteen years, he looked ancient and gnomish.

Over the court presided Pierre Mongibeaux, and, he, too, had a full sense of the theatre. He made a brief speech. 'The trial which is about to open', he said, 'is one of the greatest in history.' Beyond the door of this court there was a turmoil of passions; but 'here we know, under a triple aspect, only one passion: the passion of truth, the passion of justice and the passion of our country'. The trial began. 'Accused,' said the President, 'stand up'.

Pétain made no motion. Here was his first exposure of physical fraility: he was hard of hearing. 'Guards,' the President ordered, 'make the accused stand up.'

The prisoner stood erect. 'What are your surname, first name, age and quality?'

'Pétain, Phillippe, Marshal of France.'

The voice rang out loudly. Spectators waited eagerly to hear it again; but first Payen rose to argue that, according to the powers still vesteed in him by the National Assembly, Marshal Pétain was Head of the State. The court was not competent, therefore, to try

M

him for high treason. The President rejected the plea, and members of the jury showed their anger when Payen observed that they had not been chosen for their impartiality.

Then came the long recital of the accusation. It was too formal for the ears of laymen. They had judged already. Their minds were not open. They wanted to know what the prisoner had to say, and at last the President was ready to hear his statement. 'He can be seated, for all measures compatible with humanity and with justice shall be taken.' But the Marshal intended neither to sit nor to use glasses. He had to prove that he was fit in body as well as in mind.

Once more he stood erect. Once more his voice rang out. But he was not addressing the court, for he did not recognize its right to try him. He spoke directly to the people of France, and he began:

'Through their representatives gathered together in the National Assembly on July 10, 1940, the people of France gave me power. I have come to them to render account.

'The High Court, as it is now constituted, does not represent the people of France. The Marshal of France, Head of the State, speaks to them alone.

'I shall make no other declaration.

'I shall answer no questions. My defenders are authorized to answer the accusations which are aimed at besmirching me and which only rebound on those who make them.

'I have passed my life in the service of France. Today, cast into prison almost at the age of ninety, I wish to continue to serve her by speaking to her once again. Let her recollect! I led her armies to victory in 1918. Then, when I had earned rest, I did not cease to devote myself to her.

'I responded to all her appeals, whatever was my age or weariness.

'She turned to me on the most tragic day of her history.

'I neither sought nor desired it. I was begged to come. I came.

'Thus I inherited a catastrophe of which I was not the author.

Those who were truly responsible sheltered behind me to avert the anger of the people.

'When, in agreement with our military chiefs, I asked for an armistice I carried out a necessary and saving duty.

'Yes, the armistice saved France and contributed to the victory of the Allies by securing a free Mediterranean and the integrity of the Empire.

'Power was then legitimately vested in me and recognized by all the countries of the world, from the Holy See to the Soviet Union.

'I used the power as a buckler for protecting the French people. I went so far as to sacrifice my prestige for them. I lived at the head of a country under occupation.

'Will you understand the difficulty of governing under such conditions? Every day, with a dagger at the throat, I wrestled with the enemy's exacting demands. History will tell all that I spared you, whereas my adversaries think only of reproaching me for what was inevitable.

'The occupation compelled me to humour the enemy, but I humoured him only to enable you to take care of yourselves while waiting for the territory to be freed.

'The occupation also compelled me, against my will and against my heart, to express words and to commit acts for which I suffered more than you did, but, for all the exacting demands of the enemy, I surrendered nothing that was essential to the country's existence.

'On the contrary, I kept France together for four years by my action. I assured life and bread for the French. I assured the nation's support for our prisoners.

'Let those who accuse me and pretend to judge me ask from the depths of their conscience what, perhaps, they would have become without me.

'While General de Gaulle pursued the struggle beyond our frontiers, I prepared the ways of liberation by preserving a France stricken but alive.

'What, in fact, would have been the point of liberating ruins and cemeteries?

'By his presence on our invaded soil the enemy alone assaulted our liberties and opposed our will to rise again.

'Meanwhile I established some new institutions. The constitution which I was charged with preparing was ready, but I was unable to promulgate it.

'In spite of immense difficulties, no government has honoured the family more than mine did and sought, as a prevention of the class struggle, to guarantee conditions of work in the factory and on the land.

'Freed France can change words and names. She will reconstruct; but she will be able to reconstruct usefully only on the foundations which I have laid.

'Such examples reflect the continuity of the country, despite the partisan hatreds. No one has the right to interrupt it.

'For my part I have thought only of the union and the reconciliation of the French. Thus I spoke on the day the Germans took me away as a prisoner because they reproached me for not having ceased to fight them and for ruining their efforts.

'Now I no longer exercise power, certain people, I know, have forgotten what they said, wrote or did.

'Millions of Frenchmen are thinking of me who gave me their confidence and retain their loyalty. Neither is given to me personally, but, for them as for many others, I represent to the world a tradition which is that of the French and Christian civilization confronting the excesses of all the tyrannies.

'In condemning me, you will condemn the hope and the faith of millions of men. Thus you will aggravate or prolong the discord of France when she needs to regain her direction and good will, so that she can again take her former place among the nations.

'But my life matters little. I made France the gift of my person. At this supreme moment my sacrifice must no longer be questioned.

'If you wish to condemn me, let my condemnation be the last.

Let no other Frenchman be condemned or detained for having obeyed the orders of his lawful chief.

'But I tell you before the world that you would be condemning an innocent man, when you think you speak in the name of justice. An innocent man would sustain the burden, for a Marshal of France asks mercy of none.

'Your judgment will be confronted by that of God and of posterity. They suffice for my conscience and my memory. I leave the issue to France.'

Marshal Pétain said all that he wished to say. He had spoken to France, and not to the High Court; for he was Head of the State, he firmly believed, until the National Assembly met to withdraw the powers conferred upon him. He sat down and, treating the dock like a throne, he looked as though his eyes pierced right through the gowned and heaving bodies of his judge and accusers. There followed a strange silence. Almost at its start the trial had taken an unexpected turn; and when the President of the court broke the silence he observed sorrowfully that the attitude of the 'accused' made it difficult for him to begin an interrogation.

Indeed, interrogation was impossible, and soon there was nothing left for the President to do save to call Paul Reynaud, the first witness for the prosecution. Behind him would come the other men of the Third Republic—Daladier, Blum, Herriot, Jeanneney, Lebrun. They arrayed themselves against the men of the armistice. Those who had stood their trial at Riom or had suffered many months of unjust imprisonment were not going to be speechless in the hour of Pétain's humiliation. Unlike the prisoner, they recognized the authority of the court; but they, too, prepared their speeches so that all France might hear them. They were back again on the tribune.

Once more Reynaud spoke the language of defiance, and he did not finish until the second day of the trial drew to its close. His defence of his own actions throughout June, 1940, was brilliant and exhaustive; but, under Isorni's questionings, he admitted that the Marshal asked him to go to Washington as Ambassador and that, for a time, he had been willing to accept the mission. Daladier was gentler with the prisoner's feelings, and he spoke with a warmth and humanity which disarmed the listeners. Moreover, the treason for which he blamed Pétain was hardly full-blown, for he said: 'The Marshal betrayed the duties of his charge.' Someone, after all, had given him the charge.

Blum gave his statement a suave eloquence. He was in Paris, he said, on the eve of Reynaud's departure and, though not a member of the Government, he belonged to the ministerial circle. On the night of June 9, friends persuaded him to hurry away. Yet, two days later, he was back in Paris 'avid for news', and now it was no longer easy to track down a friend. 'I found Paris already empty, already a desert. The evacuation was already beginning.' After lunching in a little restaurant near the Madeleine he made his way to the Invalides and asked to see General Hering, who, he had supposed, was still the Military Governor of Paris. He raised a delicate protest. 'Paris is not only the capital of France, the town which symbolizes France and makes her incarnate. It is also the turn-table. There are all the communications. There are all the waterways of the Seine. All this is to be given up?' And General Hering had replied simply: 'We are waiting for a telephone call. It can come any minute.' Thus Blum left Paris, sorrowing. But the city was never empty; the tenements of anxious workers were never a desert.

One after another the men of the Third Republic made their accusations. Yet each accusing speech became obliquely a self-defence, for none were free from guilt. Unwillingly Daladier had been one of the four statesmen of Europe who imposed the Munich decree on Czechoslovakia. Reynaud had summoned Pétain from Madrid and, in the hour of defeat, named him to be his successor. Lebrun had been under no direct compulsion to ask Pétain to form a new Government. Jeanneney, as President of the Senate—like Herriot, as President of the Chamber—might have dissuaded the National Assembly from attempting a political *hari kari*. Each accuser had been himself baffled by the sweep of events.

By the easy flow of their language and by their love of the tribune they put themselves on trial again. The 'terrible' Mornet listened to them impatiently, and at last he cried: 'Let the trial of Philippe Pétain begin.' But, as Mornet knew, the prosecution had other witnesses more likely to stir the spirit of the jury. There was Michel Clemenceau, himself an old man in his seventies, who bore a likeness to his formidable father. There was also Renan's grand-daughter, Madame Henriette Psichari-Renan, and she spoke as one of the eleven thousand mothers who had lost a son in the fighting against the Americans in North Africa.

'My son hated the Germans,' she said. 'When I went to see him in Toulon in May, 1941, I asked him to come to Paris. At that time naval officers had the right to ask permission to come to Paris for forty-eight hours. He said: "Certainly, I will obtain it. I want to see my brothers, my sisters." Some time later he said: "Mother, you are in Paris. Tell me, aren't officers obliged to sal-ute German officers in the street?" I answered, "Ah, surely." He said: "Mother, I'm sorry, but I won't ask permission to go to Paris. I could never salute a German officer.' I understood.

'Our children are dead. They have died for Germany. I have two other sons who are heroes of the resistance. They have risked their lives for France. I would have said nothing if France took them away from me. I would have bowed my head, like the others. All my brothers were killed in the war. I raised my sons for France. That France should take them I accept easily, but not Germany. I submit that a chief of the Government who gave the order for eleven thousand young men to die for Germany is not a good Frenchman.'

There were many other moments of a long trial when words stirred the passions; and though Pétain seldom threw off his mask of complete detachment, he often followed the proceedings as closely as his poor hearing would allow. At the end of a difficult day Payen felt exhausted, and he asked the Marshal if he were tired. 'No, not at all,' Pétain replied. 'Besides, it's very interesting. I've learned quite a lot.' Yet there were times when the heat overcame him and when the drone of an accusing voice lulled him to sleep. He fought against this weakness, but he hated to be bored, and, at the end of another day's session, he said to Isorni: 'A bad programme today. I hope that you have got something better for tomorrow.'

On the eighth day the defence called its first witness. He was a prisoner who had come to the court from a cell in Val de Grace. A recent operation crippled him; he leaned heavily on a stick, and his face seemed to be twisted with pain. He refused, however, to be seated, and when the President of the court asked him to state his surname, his first names, his age and domicile, he replied sharply: 'Weygand, Maxim, General of the Army . . . actually a prisoner . . .'

His voice rasped as he described events from the day when Reynaud summoned him to succeed Gamelin as Commander-in-Chief to the day when Pétain asked the Germans for an armistice. He spoke as a soldier dealing with a grim situation and with an enemy capable of bending a crippled army to his will. The armistice was 'a calvary, a cross', but it was also a weapon worth seizing. In his sickness he soon wearied of addressing the court, and once the President adjourned the proceedings, so that he might rest for a quarter of an hour. Yet, when his long statement was over, he drew strength from a combat with Reynaud. He was sure of his ground, and nothing which Reynaud said could shake him. The prisoner in the makeshift dock listened intently, and then, throwing his promises to the winds, he joined in the questioning.

Resistance or armistice: which was the wiser course? The first necessity was the country's safety. And now, after five years, Reynaud was to witness another display of Weygand's abrupt anger. The statesman, Weygand complained, committed the gravest offence possible to a head of the Government: 'He lacked firmness. He did not follow the great forebears. Certainly not! Then what does he do? It is this. Freed from responsibilities, after the Assembly of July 10, at which he dared not vote—he abstained—after accepting the Marshal's invitation to go to Washington; after all this he dares to say what he does say and to accuse us—us, men like ourselves—of treason. Gentlemen, no!'

With these parting words Weygand provoked an uproar. His evidence had given a bright opening to the defence, but more witnesses of the first order were needed. Darlan was dead, and General de Gaulle prevented General Juin from coming forward, for on the day he meant to appear in the court he was ordered to inspect military units in the French zone of Germany. To disobey de Gaulle would have been to end his career in the Army.

At the eleventh hearing, moreover, there was an unexpected intervention. From time to time witnesses had mentioned Laval. He was the Marshal's 'evil genius', and nearly everyone in the court assumed that he was a fugitive in Spain. His presence, however, had become inconvenient to General Franco, and the hunted man flew to the American zone of Austria in the hope that he would find protection against revengeful compatriots. The Americans handed him to the French, who brought him to Le Bourget, and on the following day he entered the courtroom.

It was a dramatic entry. No one looked less like a former Prime Minister. The man's clothes were shabby, and his body was so shrunken that the skin hung like bags from the neck and the chin. The President had been denied his chance of interrogating Pétain, and now he would use his skill on Laval. He was soon frustrated. Laval was still a master of ambulatory utterance. He asked for a glass of water, and he made sure that he was rousing the sympathy of the onlookers. He was not the 'Marshal's evil genius'. On the contrary, he seemed to imply that he alone was the leader dogged by an 'evil genius'; and his 'evil genius' was the hero of Verdun.

Laval did not know what had been said so far in Pétain's defence; but he, too, had consented to evil things because it was necessary to deceive the enemy and to prevent him from ruling France as he ruled Poland. Foolish steps were often taken against his advice, and where he could not escape from his own responsibility he claimed that the Marshal had given approval. If he was unfair, he knew that his own life was at stake and that no plea of advanced years could save him from the executioners. He did not need the mocking glances of the jurymen—especially of those deputies who had opposed his will in the Casino at Vichy—to remind him that he was hated bitterly.

For two days he dominated the court, and he forced the Marshal once more to throw off his mask of detachment. He was questioned —it was inevitable—about a broadcast address in which, three years beforehand, he had expressed his hope of a German victory. The address, he said, had received the Marshal's approval; and indignantly Pétain rose from his chair to deny the statement. Within a crowded court Pétain's word was pitted against Laval's. Even among men tarnished with treason there were degrees of honour, and it was Laval, so many believed, who spoke falsely.

He came at last to the end of his testimony, and he walked away. As he passed Pétain's chair he halted and said: 'Farewell, Monsieur le Maréchal.' The old man was rigid. He looked straight ahead and made not the slightest acknowledgment; but the trial was never again to be freed from the shadow of an emaciated 'evil genius'.

The list of witnesses for Pétain was long. Former members of his personal staff spoke of his forbearance, courage and integrity. Some were sharing imprisonment with General Weygand, but their words were less challenging than his had been. They were unaccustomed to self-expression, and one who was trying to explain military methods drew from Pétain the impatient remark: 'Enough of tactics.'

Royalist France, too, entered the arena, but it was to speak for unity and understanding. Prince François-Xavier de Bourbon told the court how Pétain had given help to the resisters. He began his evidence by apologizing for hardness of hearing and for difficulty of speech. These impediments, he explained, were the legacies of a blow aimed at him in Dachau. Three times he had been condemned to death as a 'terrorist' or resistance worker, as a 'Communist' and as an agent for England. 'Today the Communists are in the habit of declaring a kind of monopoly, as if

they alone had been resistance workers. It must be granted that
many of them were extremely courageous, but all France was in
the resistance. You have only to open the register of the French
nobility to see how many families have lost their members,
whether in the fighting from 1939 to 1945 or in the resistance or
in the camps.'

The prince shared his camp-life with French generals who were
to be put to death. They might have often said harsh things about
the men who collaborated with the Germans, but they never spoke
ill of the Marshal, who had done all he could 'to save us, to save
those he could reach'. A companion was a doctor from Clermont
Ferrand, who had seen for himself the communal graves at Katyn
and who believed that Pétain had prevented France from becoming another Poland.

Even more moving, perhaps, was the evidence of the Abbé
Jean Rodhain. He was an Army chaplain and had been taken
prisoner on June 16, 1940. He escaped and the Marshal gave him
identity papers. Thereafter he worked secretly as a chaplain
among prisoners and the men deported for forced labour. He
entered Buchenwald, and he described a Christmas Eve which he
spent with two thousand deported Frenchmen in a fortress at
Graudens, in Poland. His Church had become the Church of the
Catacombs. 'Always it was the Marshal to whom I went for aid.'
To him alone he could speak freely.

Though pity was certainly roused by the physical frailties of
General Weygand, Pierre Laval and Prince François-Xavier de
Bourbon, the defence was wise in choosing General de Lannurien
to be its last witness for Pétain. He had been Director of the School
of War when its students included Charles de Gaulle, and in the
battle of Verdun he lost his sight. He was eloquent, and tears
streamed from his blinded eyes. 'Take care that one day—it is not,
perhaps, far distant; the drama is not yet finished—this man's
blood and alleged disgrace do not recoil on the whole of France,
on us and our children.'

Amid the cheering and the cat-calls which this speech had pro-

voked Marshal Pétain stood up. 'I wish to speak,' he said, 'I wish
to speak, just for once, to say that I am nothing here in the presence of General Lannurien. I did not even know that he wished
to come to the court. All this has been arranged without my knowledge.' And he grasped the general's hand tightly.

The procession of the witnesses was over and the way cleared
for the indictment. For six massive hours André Mornet expounded the case against Pétain. He spared the accused man nothing. Each broadcast speech, each public statement, each congratu-
latory telegram to Hitler or protesting letter to the English king
became a proof of treason. Was there a show of friendliness to the
Germans and help to the Allies? The 'double game' was false
because the help which Pétain gave was seldom, if ever, effective.
His chief desire had been to build a French authoritarian State on
the model of Nazi Germany and Fascist Italy. 'He humiliated his
country to satisfy his own desire for power.' The form was splendid. 'It is the death sentence that I demand for the man who was
Marshal Pétain.'

Without a doubt he had the jury on his side, and the manner of
his indictment so troubled Fernand Payen that he fell back on his
chosen argument of enfeebling age. Throughout the rule from
Vichy, he said, the Marshal's mind was thought to be clear for
only four or five hours a day. His hours of mental clarity belonged
to the mornings. In the evenings, therefore, members of his staff
produced the papers for him to sign; but with many nods of his
head the prisoner showed that he resented this reasoning. He
waited for Jacques Isorni to make the true defence.

This was far removed from any plea of enfeeblement, for Isorni
argued that the Marshal had sought to save the material assets of
France. Concessions were not to be avoided, since the enemy had
nearly all the cards. Many humiliations were suffered by the Marshal himself, and these he accepted, so that he might spare France
from becoming a second Poland. As a result, France had less to
endure than the other countries under military occupation. 'At
this moment when peace, civil peace, is descending upon the whole

world and the noise of war is vanishing, ' Isorni cried at last, 'do not wound any more the holy soil of France. Judges of the High Court, listen to me. Hear my appeal. You are only judges. You are only judging a man. But you carry in your hands the destiny of France.'

It was already after eleven o'clock when, on the evening of August 14, Pétain rose to utter his last public words.

'Throughout the trial,' he said, 'I have kept silence voluntarily after explaining to the French people the reasons for my attitude. My thought, my only thought, was to remain with them on the soil of France, according to my promise, so as to protect them and to lessen their sufferings. Whatever comes, they will not forget. They know I defended them as I defended Verdun. Judges, my life and freedom are in your hands, but I confide my honour to the country. Dispose of me according to your consciences. Mine does not reproach me at all, for during a life already long and now brought by my age to the threshold of the grave I affirm that I have no other ambition than that of serving France.'

As soon as the prisoner had finished the court rose. Journalists and barristers made for a buffet within the Palace of Justice, and the Marshal walked slowly to the robing-room which he shared with his wife. There he found Canon Potteville, chaplain at Montrouge, waiting for him. 'Are you satisfied with me, Canon?' he asked.

'Oh, Monsieur le Maréchal!'

'But God, is He satisfied with me?'

A few minutes later it was midnight, and in his wife's company Pétain heard Mass. Afterwards he rested on his bed and spoke little. He was calm, contented and ready for the sentence of death.

From the buffet came the hubbub of talk. All over Paris cafés were doing a brisk business, for a microphone had been fixed to the President's desk, and the radio would transmit the decree of the High Court. The hour belonged to the men of the resistance.

Yet the sentence of death was not a certainty. Where lay the treason? Time dragged on; there was, perhaps, no unanimous decision. Something might happen to save a Marshal from the bullets. New light might play upon the ugly, but receding, record of Vichy. Peace, Isorni had said, was 'descending upon the whole world'; but it was disturbing peace. The Allies had dropped atomic bombs on Hiroshima and Nagasaki and, as it happened, the day of judgment on Pétain was the day of surrender in the Far East. A new weapon of warfare seemed to rob final victory of its moral lustre. The burden of guilt fell on the many, and not merely on the few.

It was nearly four o'clock in the morning when a bell rang, and a crowd swept out of the buffet and into the courtroom which, save for the lights round the President's desk, was kept almost in darkness. The Marshal sat too far away to hear the President, who spoke for twenty minutes before pronouncing the decree. Pétain was condemned to death, to national infamy and to the confiscation of his goods; but 'taking into account the great age of the accused man the High Court of Justice expresses the wish that the condemnation to death shall not be carried out'.

'Guards,' the President said, 'take the condemned man away.'

The trial was ended. Sadly Pétain said farewell to his wife, to Isorni and Lemaire. A black prison-van drove him to the Orly airport. It was the first stage of a long journey to the fortress of Portalet, near the Pyrenees. He had sacrificed a night's sleep to receive the death sentence, and two days were to pass before he heard that he had been reprieved. Yet his ironic humour did not desert him. He was brought into contact with the administrator of prisons, whose name was Amor.

'Amor?' he said. 'So am I.'

The prisoner spent three months in Portalet before he was taken to Ile d'Yeu, an Atlantic island a few miles off the rugged coast of the Vendée. Here his cell opened directly to a large compound, but grey outer walls blocked all views of the sea. Simon, who had gone with him to Portalet, was still his custodian, and though, as a loyal servant of the State, he imposed the penitentiary rules, he hid neither his admiration nor his pity. Soon strong bonds of sympathy drew the prisoner to his three guards—Miot, Brendart and Roy, who was a Communist. In the small and simple Hotel des Voyageurs lived Madame Pétain. She was now in her late sixties and suffered from sciatica, but daily she trod the hard, wind-swept road which leads from Port-Joinville to the citadel. She made the cake which—on April 24, 1946—bore the burden of ninety candles.

On the previous night Isorni and Lemaire arrived at the Hotel des Voyageurs, so that they might be the prisoner's guests at his birthday party. They were now the guardians of his honour. They took no fee, and they promised never to rest until the Marshal's rehabilitation had been secured. As they sat in the hotel they saw people coming shyly to Madame Pétain with small presents for her husband, and while they were on their way to the citadel, a man asked them to wait for a moment. He entered his homestead and came out with a half-pound of butter. 'Give this to the Marshal,' he said, 'on behalf of a peasant.'

Pétain welcomed his guests eagerly, He seemed to be little changed, and he was ready to enter into the spirit of a party; but the story of the half-pound of butter touched him. For a while he was silent. Then he said: 'It must be shared with the guards.'

Over the modest feast of coffee and birthday-cake Pétain asked: 'What has become of de Gaulle? That interests me. The boy is intelligent, very intelligent, even when he oversteps the mark.'

'Monsieur le Maréchal, he quitted office when the difficulties multiplied.'

'That doesn't surprise me. I, on the contrary, am at home when things become more difficult. Besides, de Gaulle has only done this in order to get back. I know him well. He has had his fill of battle and takes himself for Napoleon.'

'A Napoleon who would have won no battles.'

'Yes, but he commented very well on mine . . . I condemned him. He condemned me. Indeed, we are both condemned.'

Isorni mentioned Churchill.

'Churchill,' Pétain broke in, 'now there's somebody. He is not distinguished in his manner, but in his mind. He seeemed to understand me. After the talk we walked round the garden. Churchill took my arm in a friendly way. "Then, Marshal, you will come with us?" I told him that I could not. My duty was to remain with the French in their misfortune. Churchill expressed his regret. But he really seemed to understand me. Yes, and even to approve of me.'

But there was one man about whom Pétain refused to say a word. That man was the dead Laval. He could not speak in praise and he would not caluminate. He chose silence.

At length he said: 'You don't know how I suffer. I suffer terribly, even when I say nothing and, above all, when I try to keep smiling. But I suffer without self-pity. I will never go in for self-pity.'

'Monsieur le Maréchal, you said some years ago that the most necessary form of courage was patience.'

'I am patient. I accept everything.'

'You must let the time of hatred go by.'

'Hatred? I don't understand hatred. I have never tried it. For me hatred is too complicated. Do you believe that France really needs my rehabilitation?'

'It will be a necessity for her.'

'Don't forget, if I have not already spoken to you about it, that you must ask for it even after my death.'

'We have thought of that.'

'Ah, you have already foreseen my death.'

Each morning the prisoner saw the three guards hoisting the tricolour to the top of a flagpole, and each evening he saw them bringing it down. They were small ceremonies, but he was a traditionalist. He took pleasure in the growing warmth of summer and a guard who had planted some tomatoes in the compound shouted: 'Look, Monsieur le Maréchal, they are getting red.' 'Yes,' he replied, 'with shame.'

The weeks of incarceration turned into years. The prisoner lost the habit of sleep and, when he was 93, there came a sharp decline in his mental and physical powers. 'I've had enough, enough,' Simon heard him saying.

One day Isorni visited the cell to find the prisoner discussing affairs of State with Simon. 'We must settle this question of the Fleet.' And Simon replied: 'Leave the Fleet alone. We have no more ships.'

Yet as soon as Simon had gone Pétain got back his lucidity. 'Get me out of here, I beg you,' he said to Isorni. 'Sometimes I put on the air of lucidity. But all this is disgraceful. Truly disgraceful. You don't know what it means to be deprived of freedom.'

Isorni and Lemaire were doing their best. They approached President Auriol. They asked for the support of the French Academy, and they helped Louis Madelin to launch an influential committee. Madame Pétain went on begging for permission to live in the citadel and to share her husband's privations. Prisoners at Fresnes asked that their own detention might be prolonged so as to shorten Pétain's; and General de Gaulle, who had taken care that the condemned man should not face the firing squad, now pleaded for his freedom. But the machine of government mocked humanity and, in 1949, Pétain's goods were put up for auction.

There were, indeed, tardy changes within the citadel; it became less of a prison and more of a hospital. Miot, Brandart and Roy—the guards to whom Pétain had become devoted—were removed. Simon left Ile d'Yeu to become director of the prison at La Roquette. Life behind the forbidding walls was less penal, but it was also lonelier.

From time to time reports that Pétain was dying brought journalists to the island, and functionaries went into committee to decide what was to happen at his death. The body, it was decreed, must be clothed in civilian dress and buried within the citadel. Only the family and the two defending barristers could attend the Mass 'with the body present', though journalists and 'friends' were free to go to a Mass in the church of Port-Joinville. In a desire to be helpful the prefecture of the Vendée sent a coffin to the island, and for more than a year it remained only a few yards from Pétain's cell.

By the spring of 1951 Pétain was so ill and frail that few ex-

N

pected him to see his ninety-fifth birthday. Yet Madame Pétain made the cake and ordered the candles, and for a brief hour the aged man enjoyed his party.

Now the people were shamed by a martyrdom. Soldiers were ordered to decorate and to get ready a small one-floored house in Port-Joinville, and when Pétain heard the news he thanked the two barristers. 'You are like brothers,' he told them. 'I hope you will be so always.'

They were his last lucid words. On June 29 he was taken from the citadel. Freedom came, but the mind had gone, and on the morning of July 23 the warrior's life drew to its close. The orders which the functionaries had issued were no longer valid. Loving hands dressed the dead man in his Marshal's uniform and pinned his Military Medal on the breast. Men of Verdun and former prisoners-of-war took the body from the house to the church and from the church to the graveyard.

There, perhaps, it will rest until the last defender of Verdun is dead and a more pitying generation remembers a hero's wish to be buried in the cemetery of Douaumont among the thousands who, in their prime or their youth, died fighting for France.

INDEX